A PROCESS GUIDE FOR SCHOOL IMPROVEMENT

Herbert J. Klausmeier

UNIVERSITY
PRESS OF
AMERICA

LANHAM • NEW YORK • LONDON

Library of Congress Cataloging in Publication Data

Klausmeier, Herbert J. (Herbert John), 1915-
    A process guide for school improvement.

    Bibliography: p.
    1. School improvement programs—Handbooks, manuals,
etc.   2. School improvement programs—Wisconsin—Case
studies.   I. Title.
LB2822.8.K53   1985   379.1'54   85-20193
ISBN 0-8191-4941-1 (alk. paper)
ISBN 0-8191-4942-X (pbk. : alk. paper)

The research reported in this paper was funded by the Wisconsin
Center for Education Research which is supported in part by a grant
from the National Institute of Education (Grant No. NIE-G-84-0008).
The opinions expressed in this paper do not necessarily reflect the
position, policy, or endorsement of the National Institute of Education.
Support for the production of this *Guide* was provided by the School
of Education, University of Wisconsin-Madison, and the Faye
McBeath Foundation, Milwaukee, WI.

Co-published by arrangement with
The Wisconsin Center for Education Research

Acknowledgments

I express my thanks to the persons who contributed in many different ways to this Guide. Personnel of schools and the central offices of Ashwaubenon, Cedarburg, and Milwaukee, Wisconsin, participated with me in cooperative improvement research from 1982 to 1985. This and earlier research from 1977 to 1982 identified how the schools and the central office of a district working together develop and institutionalize a self-improvement capability in each school of the district.

Personnel of many other districts participated in school improvement workshops that started in 1982. They, too, provided much information regarding the implementation of the improvement strategies and the facilitative components of schooling described in this Guide.

I am especially grateful to the following Wisconsin schools and districts for the exemplary practices that show how they implemented the strategies and components: Ashwaubenon High School, Green Bay; Auer Avenue Elementary School, Milwaukee; Burroughs Middle School, Milwaukee; Cedarburg High School, Cedarburg; Eighth Street Middle School, Milwaukee; Franklin High School, Franklin; James Madison High School, Milwaukee; John Audubon Middle School, Milwaukee; Morse Middle School, Milwaukee; Parkview Elementary School, Cedarburg; Parkview High School, Orfordville; Phoenix Middle School, Delavan; Richard Kluge Elementary School, Milwaukee; Steuben Middle School, Milwaukee; Stevens Point Area High School, Stevens Point; Washington High School, Milwaukee; Webster Transitional School, Cedarburg; William Horlick High School, Racine; Cedarburg School District, Cedarburg; Milwaukee School District, Milwaukee.

Many organizations participated in a state-wide diffusion process: the Association of Wisconsin School Administrators; the Wisconsin Association of School District Administrators; the Wisconsin Department of Public Instruction; and seven state universities: UW --Eau Claire, La Crosse, Madison, Milwaukee, Oshkosh, Platteville, and Stevens Point.

John Daresh, now at Ohio State University, was a coauthor of two editions of a secondary school improvement manual that preceded this Guide; and Julie McGivern, now completing her Ph.D. studies, was a coauthor of the first manual. I am pleased to recognize their contributions to the earlier manuals and wish that I could have employed them as coauthors of this Guide.

I was able to employ Tom Pautsch, Principal of Webster Transitional School, and Fritz Turner, Director of Pupil Services, McFarland School District, as practitioner consultants in preparing this Guide. They helped me generate the chapter organization and reviewed some of the final chapter drafts. Tom prepared a first draft of parts of Chapters 1 and 2 and Fritz did the same for Chapter 12. Their practitioner views are reflected throughout the Guide. Professor James Lipham reviewed the entire Guide and provided many helpful suggestions.

Debbie Stewart, who heads the Center's Dissemination Office, copyedited the manuscript. Teri Frailey, with assistance from Elvira Benter and Arlene Knudsen, did the word processing and typing. The Wisconsin Center administration and support personnel were helpful in many ways, including the final production of this Guide. The contributions of all the Center persons, and especially Maureen Ormson and her staff who operate the duplication shop, are deeply appreciated.

Continuing support from the Wisconsin Center for Education Research enabled me to synthesize my two decades of elementary and secondary school improvement research and to put it into this Guide in a form that practitioners can readily use.

I thank the Faye McBeath Foundation for its monetary contribution to the preparation and distribution of this Guide.

Recognition is due to the School of Education and the University of Wisconsin-Madison that permitted me through a chaired professorship to devote most of the second semester of the 1984-85 academic year to the preparation of this Guide.

The publisher, University Press of America, merits our deep appreciation for producing this high quality book within a period of two months and for keeping the retail price at a very minimum. University Press also published a theoretical book--The Renewal and Improvement of Secondary Education: Concepts and Practices, 1983-- and a report of improvement research--Developing and Institutionalizing a Self-Improvement Capability, 1985. The first book provides a theoretical model and the second one the research evidence underlying the detailed suggestions for improving secondary schooling given in this Guide. (Similar supplementary sources of information for elementary schooling are listed in the Appendix.)

Herbert J. Klausmeier
May 1, 1985

Contents

How To Use This Guide.

Chapter 1
Implementing Basic Improvement Processes:
Every School Can.

Chapter 2
Administering School Improvement:
Dynamic Leadership.

Chapter 3
Arranging Total Educational Programs for Students:
A Helping Hand. 45

Chapter 4
Improving Instruction:
Teacher Involvement Is the Key. 61

Chapter 5
Updating the Curriculum: An Annual Priority.83

Chapter 6
Student Decision-Making Arrangements, Self-Discipline, and Citizenship: Democracy Includes Students, Too. 99

Chapter 7
Evaluation and Improvement Strategies: Using Information Constructively .113

Chapter 8
Organizing Students and Teachers for Instruction: It's Time To Replace 19th Century Patterns .129

Chapter 9
Personalizing Educational Advising:
How To Combat the 250:1 Ratio. 143

Chapter 10
Strengthening Home-School-Community Relations:
Parents, Business, and Labor Participate. 165

ix

Chapter 11

Guiding Improvement Through Locally Conducted
Research: Effective Schools Are Doing It . 183

Chapter 12

Implementing Improvement Processes
In Elementary Schools:
Successful Schooling Begins Here . 199

x

Appendix
Correlated Instructional Materials and Their Uses in Locally Conducted Inservice Programs

About the Author

How To Use This Guide

This <u>Guide</u> is for use in locally conducted inservice programs and in university credit courses and noncredit programs. It is designed to aid each school of a district and the district office itself in starting and maintaining a self-improvement capability. A school that has developed a self-improvement capability is able to:

maintain student outcomes (knowledge and understanding, skill and competence, attitude and interest, and action patterns and citizenship) that are already satisfactory and better those that are not;

maintain already effective instructional, advising, and administrative practices and better those that are not;

maintain already high job satisfaction and staff morale and raise it if not high; and

increase the competencies and professional development of the staff, thereby achieving renewal as a social organization.

This <u>Guide</u> replaces a 1983 <u>Secondary School Improvement Manual</u> and has been written to be easily used by any school as follows. Chapter 1 of this 1985 <u>Guide</u> is for all levels of schooling, Chapters 2 through 11 are more for the middle school and high school, and Chapter 12 is more for the elementary school. Although certain chapters address one level of schooling more than another, local school persons and district officials interested in the continuity of schooling might well study all of the chapters.

The order for studying the chapters is important. Persons interested mainly in secondary schooling should read Chapters 1 and 2 first and then turn to any other chapter of highest immediate interest. Persons interested mainly in elementary schooling should start with Chapter 1 and then go to Chapter 12.

Another item is critical. Chapters 2 through 11 give improvement suggestions and illustrative exemplary practices of both middle schools and high schools; Chapter 12 does the same for elementary schools. Most of the information regarding the middle schools is relevant for elementary schooling and vice versa. Accordingly, examine the contents to identify middle school or elementary school practices of interest.

A school staff usually starts an improvement program pertaining more to one component of schooling than another. Accordingly, in some schools only Guide Chapter 1 and the chapter pertaining to the component of interest are studied in detail by all the staff. For this reason, some schools duplicate and distribute only the chapters of immediate interest. While this is appropriate, having a few copies of the Guide in the schools' professional library so that staff members can study any chapter of interest is a wise procedure.

Although most schools require no printed material other than this Guide, two other kinds of material may prove helpful. First, simulations are available from the Wisconsin Center for Education Research: one set for elementary school, another for middle school, and one for high school. The simulations are designed to aid a committee identify possible broad areas of improvement, clarify individual committee members' roles and responsibilities, and use test information in prioritizing improvement projects. The simulations are also designed to encourage open communication among committee members and to enable them to ascertain the extent to which they agree regarding critical issues related to school improvement. Second, supplementary materials for both secondary schooling and elementary schooling are provided in the Appendix. The Appendix also gives detailed suggestions for using this Guide in locally conducted inservice/staff development programs. The suggestions include time schedules during regular school hours. These suggestions should be read before attempting to start a school improvement program since teachers must have time to prepare for planning and implementing any improvement project.

I hope that practitioners and others who seek the improvement of education will find this Guide helpful both immediately and in the years ahead. Developing a self-improvement capability and simultaneously finding the means for self-renewal is not easy. However, it is a most practical means of advancing the cause of effective schooling for all American children and youth.

Chapter 1
Implementing Basic Improvement Processes: Every School Can

Rationale

A Design for Improving Schooling

The Design and School Effectiveness

**What Does the District Office Do
To Start Its Self-Improvement Capability?**

**What Does a School Do
To Start Its Self-Improvement Capability?**

Developing the Annual Improvement Plan

**Improvement Plan—Improving Grade 10 English
Achievement, 1983-84: Cedarburg High School, Cedarburg, WI**

Providing Internal and External Support

Formulating District Guidelines

**District Guidelines for
Annual School Improvement Planning, 1984-85:
Cedarburg School District, Cedarburg, WI**

Rationale

Can individual schools develop a capability for improving their own educative processes from year to year? The pioneering staffs of some elementary schools, middle schools, and high schools have done so in recent years. They were creative, worked exceptionally hard, and persisted. They learned to carry out a key goal-based improvement strategy and other primary improvement strategies. They are refining these strategies each year. And by use of the strategies, they readily put relevant effective-school characteristics into practice.

Can other schools develop a self-improvement capability with less effort and fewer frustrations? They can when they are stimulated and aided properly by the district office. Moreover, school districts that have developed improvement guidelines not only aid each school of the district in developing a capability, they also help the schools maintain and refine the capability. Accordingly, effective practices aren't dropped when the principal or the superintendent leaves; nor are changed priorities permitted to wipe out hard-earned improvements.

The strategies and processes by which all the schools of a district and the district office itself readily establish a self-improvement capability are incorporated in a design for school improvement. This chapter introduces the design; later chapters spell out the step-by-step procedures that schools have successfully employed in implementing it.

A Design for Improving Schooling

The design represents a synthesis of the best practices that school staffs and I have identified through many years of cooperative improvement research. The design and its relationship to the district guidelines are shown in Figure 1.1.

The district administrator and key staff, supported by the school board, take initiative for forming the district improvement committee. In smaller school districts, this is not a new committee. Rather, the existing administrative council takes on the school improvement responsibility. However, it is appropriate not to have a majority of the principal members from any one level of schooling. In middle-size districts, the committee includes the district administrator and representative principals from each school level. In large school districts, the membership includes

3

Figure 1.1 A Design for Starting and Maintaining a Self-Improvement Capability in Each School and in the District Office

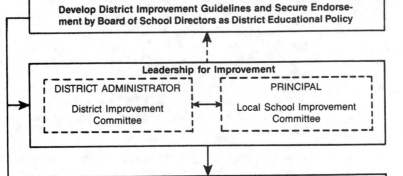

Develop District Improvement Guidelines and Secure Endorsement by Board of School Directors as District Educational Policy

Leadership for Improvement

DISTRICT ADMINISTRATOR

District Improvement Committee

PRINCIPAL

Local School Improvement Committee

Implement Basic Improvement Strategy (Goal-Based Strategy):

- Assess present status
- Identify already satisfactory outcomes and already effective strategies and components to be maintained and identify others to be improved
- Develop a plan for each area to be improved
- Implement the planned activities and monitor progress
- Evaluate the effectiveness of the activities

Implement Two Primary Improvement Strategies:

Arrange an effective total educational program of curricular and extracurricular offerings for each student (individual educational programming strategy). ↔ Arrange an effective instructional program for each student in each course (individual instructional programming strategy).

Direct Strategies Toward Attaining These Goals:

- Maintain student outcomes (knowledge and understanding, skill and competence, attitude and value, action patterns and citizenship) that are already satisfactory and improve those that are not.
- Maintain already high staff morale and job satisfaction and raise it if not high.

Modify School Components as Necessary to Implement the Strategies:

- Curriculum
- Instruction
- Student Decision Making
- Evaluation of Student Learning and the School's Educational Programs
- Administrative Structures and Processes

- Organization of Students and Teachers for Instruction
- Organization of Students and Teachers for Student Advisement
- Home-School-Community Relations

the deputy or assistant superintendent, one or two other key district officials, and representative principals. In very large districts, the principals may have a separate committee that serves in an advisory relationship to the district office committee.

The district committee develops the district's improvement guidelines. At the outset, principals provide input to the district officials in formulating the guidelines. Moreover, the district committee arranges for all the principals of the district and each school staff to review the guidelines before the guidelines are forwarded to the school board. When endorsing the guidelines, board members recognize that substantial revisions may be made after the first year or two of districtwide implementation.

The guidelines indicate how the improvement committee is to be formed at each school level. In the high school, the committee consists of the principal and the chairs, or teachers, of part or all of the departments or broad fields. In the middle school, the membership consists of the principal and representative teachers. The representative teachers may be from teaching teams, broad fields, or departments. In the elementary school, the committee is the principal and representative teachers from grades or from teams of teachers. Typically, the IMC director, a counselor, and a special education teacher are members of the committee at all school levels.

The basic goal-based improvement strategy is implemented annually with assistance from the district in line with the provisions of the district guidelines. Briefly the goal-based strategy involves assessing present status, identifying areas to be improved, setting improvement goals and developing a plan to attain sets of goals pertaining to each area, implementing the planned activities, monitoring progress in implementing the activities, evaluating the effectiveness of the activities, and using the results of the evaluation in identifying needs and developing plans for the ensuing year.

The two primary improvement strategies—individual educational programming and individual instructional programming—are closely related. Both focus on the individual student rather than on all the students of a class, a grade, or the whole school as an undifferentiated group.

Schools arrange an effective total educational program of curricular and cocurricular offerings for each student by (a) providing relevant course offerings, (b) making sure that each student is placed in appropriate courses, and (c) providing the students good instruction in each course. Schools that are arranging an appropriate instructional program for each student in each course ensure first that each course is appropriate for the student; and, second, that the instruction in each course is designed to enable the student to attain relevant course objectives, to learn well, and to spend the entire class period in active learning.

To implement the two primary strategies effectively, many schools have found it necessary to change their organization for instruction and advising. When starting to implement the goal-based strategy, all schools modify or refine their administrative structure and processes to include teachers and, in turn, to increase communication between administrators and teachers and among teachers of different grades and different departments or broad fields.

The goal of school improvement is not to implement a strategy or to have a certain school component functioning in a particular way. Rather, it is to attain desired student outcomes and staff outcomes. As noted in Figure 1.1, the foremost goal is maintaining already high student outcomes--knowledge and understanding, skill and competence, attitudes and values, action patterns, and citizenship--and improving those that are not. The second goal is to ensure that staff morale and job satisfaction are high. As each school, with district support, attains these goals from year to year, it achieves renewal as a social organization, develops and maintains a self-improvement capability. As the district office provides leadership and support, it too develops its self-improvement capability.

The basic improvement strategy is explained in this chapter. A separate chapter is given to administrative arrangements, each primary improvement strategy, and each schooling component given in Figure 1.1.

The Design and School Effectiveness

The Wisconsin Department of Public Instruction in February of 1985 endorsed the following characteristics of effective schools:

1. Strong instructional leadership.
2. Clear school mission and accompanying instructional program.
3. High expectations for students.
4. An orderly school learning climate.
5. Opportunity to learn and an emphasis on academic learning time.
6. Frequent monitoring of pupil progress.
7. High degree of parent/community involvement.

The Department indicated that putting these characteristics into practice "makes schools more effective because they help teachers and administrators provide better instruction and help students to retain and learn more information."

This approach to school effectiveness is quite similar to other descriptions of school effectiveness. It defines an effective school as one that has all of the preceding characteristics. It concentrates on instructional leadership, academic instruction, student academic achievement, a safe learning environment and classrooms free of discipline problems, and participation by parents and the community. Like other accounts of effective schooling, it does not directly mention the role of the district office nor does it indicate with any specificity the means by which an ineffective school changes its practices and becomes effective. Finally, criteria for determining the extent to which a school is effective are not indicated, other than that the school is practicing the effectiveness characteristics.

A quick comparison of the seven characteristics and Figure 1.1 shows that any of the seven characteristics could be identified as a weak area of a school, to be improved through application of the basic improvement strategy shown in Figure 1.1.

What Does the District Office Do To Start Its Self-Improvement Capability?

Designates the district office person who leads and coordinates the district improvement activities.

Establishes a districtwide improvement committee consisting of district officials and representative elementary, middle, and high school principals, a school board member, and possibly teachers and counselors. The committee:

Develops guidelines, endorsed by the school board, that are designed to ensure the orderly development and institutionalization of the improvement capability in the district office and in each school.

Aids each local school in implementing the guidelines.

What Does a School Do
To Start Its Self-Improvement Capability?

The principal proceeds in accordance with district guidelines if they are available. If they are not available, the principal moves ahead after securing district office and school board support. The principal either establishes an Educational Improvement Committee (EIC) that is responsible for leading and coordinating the school's improvement activities or delegates the improvement responsibility to an existing group or groups. This committee (schools call it by different names) includes the principal and/or other members of the administrative team and representative teachers and counselors.

The improvement committee carries out the following improvement process:

Phase 1: Makes the staff aware of the need for establishing a self-improvement capability and builds staff commitment.

Phase 2: Uses available assessment information and gathers others, if necessary, to ascertain the extent to which the school's educational goals are being attained, and identifies and prioritizes areas of improvement annually.

Phase 3: Develops an improvement plan for each selected area of improvement annually.

Phase 4: Ensures that the relevant staff is properly prepared to implement the planned activities before starting the implementation.

Phase 5: Implements the planned activities and monitors progress.

Phase 6: Evaluates the effectiveness of the improvement activities annually and reports the results of the evaluation annually.

Phase 7: Repeats the cycle annually, starting with Phase 2, in refining the improved practices.

Phase 1: Awareness and Commitment

The district guidelines provide the essential information that the EIC of each school needs in making the entire staff aware of

8

the nature of a school's self-improvement capability and in securing staff commitment. Among other things, the guidelines indicate the role of the staff in implementing all of the remaining phases of the process, and they specify the kinds of assistance the district provides. Accordingly, the staff does not debate whether to start but focuses on when, where, and how to start. Enthusiasm and commitment by the EIC and a well-planned program of staff awareness and commitment are the essentials of implementing Phase 1.

Phase 2: Assessment and Needs Identification

School improvement starts with using available assessment information and gathering other information as necessary to identify strengths and possible weaknesses. One main type of information used in identifying strengths and weaknesses pertains to student outcomes as reflected by attendance, test scores, and teacher opinions. Strengths to be maintained and areas to be improved are identified both for individual students and for groups of students, such as all of those of a grade.

Phase 3: Planning

Planning follows needs identification. Great progress follows from careful planning. Conversely, failure, accompanied with much teacher frustration, occurs when projects are started without adequate planning. Success of improvement projects is enhanced through adherence to the following propositions regarding the planning process:

School improvement doesn't just happen. It needs to be planned and planning itself needs to be planned for.

Ownership is important. The people who are going to do the work should be involved in problem identification, planning the solution, implementing the planned activities, monitoring progress, and evaluating the outcomes.

There are no universal solutions. Rather, there are multiple ways to resolve an educational problem. And, the right way to resolve a problem depends on the physical, social, and economic characteristics of each particular school.

The staffs of most schools have the knowledge and skills to identify and solve the educational problems of their school.

9

Different roles, responsibility, and authority are possessed by individuals of a school staff. And, resolving educational problems requires the full utilization of everyone's knowledge and skills.

The administrative leader's responsibility in planning is that of organizing and facilitating the work of the staff.

Educational planning is directed toward attaining the school's overriding goal: the academic, civic, social, and psychological growth of each student.

Educational planning recognizes that parents want each child to experience success and want to be kept informed of the child's progress. Accordingly, a caring adult plans the child's educational program with the child and his or her parents, monitors the child's progress to ensure success, and confers with the parents on a regular basis.

Educational planning recognizes that parents, school board members, and others in the community want to be informed of how effective their school is. The school provides this information to the public on an annual basis. In reports to the public, the privacy of every child, every teacher, and every administrator is carefully protected.

Phase 4: Preparation

Preparation of the staff for implementing a planned improvement begins when the needs of the staff for gaining information or for developing skills or materials have been identified. Illustrative preparation activities include school visits, workshops, conferences, studying this Guide and other materials, and procuring or developing materials for student or teacher use.

It is critical that all staff members have sufficient time to prepare for implementation. Schools that are preparing to implement two or more comprehensive improvement projects typically devote all of their inservice and staff development time to preparing for the implementation.

Phase 5: Implementing Planned Activities
and Monitoring Progress

Implementation of the planned activities commences as closely as possible to the time they are scheduled to begin. Most activities that are given in the plans included in this Guide start at the beginning of the school year and end toward the close of the year. However, Chapter 12 presents one project that was planned during the first two months of the school year, implemented during the next six months, and evaluated in the ninth month (May).

Monitoring progress starts early, not later than the end of the first grading period. The primary purposes of the monitoring are to identify and overcome difficulties and to confirm the desired performances of students, staff, or both.

Phase 6: Evaluation and Reporting

Evaluation of the effectiveness of the current year's improvement activities starts at the same time as the monitoring, and it continues throughout the year. Usually the data collected are summarized shortly after the school year ends.

The evaluation information gathered throughout the year is summarized, reported, and used in setting goals and planning related improvement activities for the ensuing year.

Phase 7: Refinement and Institutionalization

Refinement of improved practices occurs as the basic and primary improvement strategies indicated in Figure 1.1 are implemented from one year to the next. Most improvements require three years to become fixed, or institutionalized.

As teachers and other school staff gain more knowledge and increase their skills in attaining the desired student outcomes indicated in Figure 1.1, they experience renewal as a social organization. Simultaneously, the school develops its own self-improvement capability.

Here are a few tips for ensuring success in starting an improvement program:

Start with what seems to be relatively small scale. Most projects require two or three times more effort than is initially anticipated.

Select a project or two where the likelihood of successful implementation and positive results is high. For example, it is easier to eliminate interruptions of class time from external sources than to eliminate discipline problems.

Involve the whole staff. To illustrate, improving attendance involves more of the staff than raising grade 8 achievement in mathematics.

Keep enthusiasm high. For example, celebrate the attainment of each project milestone during the school year with informal rap sessions in the teachers' lounge.

Developing the Annual Improvement Plan

The planning process is clarified by presenting a completed plan. The format of the plan is used by elementary schools, middle schools, high schools, and district offices. Comments after some of the completed items elaborate the planning process.

Improvement Plan—Improving Grade 10 English Achievement, 1983-84: Cedarburg High School, Cedarburg, WI

1. Area of Improvement

   Improvement of 10th grade English achievement, 1983-84.

2. Need for Improvement

   The achievement of some 9th grade students in certain English skills as assessed by a standardized test was found by the instructional coordinator and English teachers to be lower than desired. Accordingly, the English curriculum was examined to ascertain whether the skills in which the students were low were included in the curriculum. Since they were, the teachers decided that interventions would be appropriate in the skills showing the greatest numbers of low-achieving students. Interventions were begun the following fall in grade 10 since the achievement test was given in the spring in grade 9.

3. Percent of Students and Grades Involved

   100% of the grade 10 class.

4. Persons Who Planned and Will Coordinate and Evaluate the Project

   The Educational Improvement Committee (EIC) which includes the principal, instructional coordinator, IMC director, reading specialist, a counselor, and one teacher from each department.

Comment: The larger the student enrollment, the more likely there will be task forces rather than only one EIC. More task forces are found in high schools than in middle schools or elementary schools because of the more specialized nature of the high school curriculum and high school teachers' interests.

5. Persons Who Will Implement the Project

   Principal, instructional coordinator, guidance counselors, chairperson of the English department, all teachers of grade 10 English, and all teacher advisors of all grade 10 students.

6. Improvement Goals

General Goal

   High English achievement by grade 10 students individually and as a group will be maintained and low achievement will be raised.

Performance Goals

   Each 10th-grade student's English achievement as measured by the Comprehensive Tests of Basic Skills will be as high as or higher than his/her ability level as measured by the Test of Cognitive Skills, and as high as or higher than it was in grade 9.

   The English subscores of the 10th-grade students as a group as measured by the Comprehensive Tests of Basic Skills will be as high as or higher than the group's ability level as measured by the Test of Cognitive Skills.

Comment: Purposive cognitive psychology and experience in all areas of human endeavor make three things clear: First, having a goal determines the direction of our activities. Second, intending to attain the goal keeps us on task until the goal is achieved. Third, the more realistic the goal and the better our plans for achieving it, the more likely we will in fact achieve it. Typically, a school sets general goals for its first projects, for example, student attendance will be higher in 1986-87 than it was in 1985-86. With experience, a more specific performance goal is set; for example, student attendance will increase from 94% to 96%.

Better results are obtained when the specific goal is set. The specific goal implies a clear expectation, and it is more easily monitored. Weight watchers recognize that it is easier to lose two pounds in one month than to lose weight for one month.

There is considerable hesitancy to set measurable performance goals. Teachers, and principals too, feel that they personally have failed if a goal is not attained. They also fear being evaluated negatively. To counteract this hesitancy, educators and the public should recognize that a goal statement is an estimate of performance and an indicator of intent, not a contract. A goal should not be considered as a contract because there are many uncontrollable factors in the school setting and the educational community that affect students' performances and interfere with goal attainment. When a goal is not attained, the constructive response is to try to identify the causes and correct the situation rather than to blame self or to be negatively and unfairly evaluated. Clearly, those who evaluate teachers' or principals' performances must honor this point if realistic goal setting is to occur in a school.

7. Preparatory Activities Including Staff Development/Inservice

2 1/2 day off-site workshop (Wisconsin Program for the Renewal and Improvement of Secondary Education) for 4 EIC members, including instructional coordinator and chair of English Department.

1/2 day onsite inservice for all grade 10 English teachers to identify skill areas in which the mean achievement of all students is low and to work out remedial techniques.

1/2 day onsite inservice for all grade 10 English teachers and all grade 10 teacher advisors to gain a better understanding of the Comprehensive Tests of Basic Skills from a representative of the test publisher.

1/2 day onsite inservice for all grade 10 English teachers and all grade 10 teacher advisors to clarify the advising and goal-setting process to be employed in individual conferences with students.

14

Comment: The amount of preparation required prior to implementation is directly related to the scope of the project and the competence of the implementers in carrying out the required new or refined practices. Regardless of these factors, for success on any project the teaching schedules of the EIC and of the implementers are arranged so that they can meet at regular times during the school day and outside school hours as necessary.

District administrators and school boards tend to underestimate the amount of preparation time greatly. Moreover, education in comparison with business and industry is notorious for not providing adequately for the initial preparation and the continuing education of teachers. Accordingly, teachers' class schedules, overall job responsibilities, and use of time throughout the required hours at school require careful analysis before undertaking a major improvement project. Most schools find that a considerable number of hours per week can be found for teacher preparation.

8. First-Year Implementation Activities and Monitoring Progress

The grade 10 English teachers will implement English instruction in the manner in which it was designed in 1981-82. In 1981-82 objective-based curricula were written for all English classes.

Implementation Activities

Students enrolled in different sections of the same grade 10 course will receive instruction on the same objectives and will be given a common final exam. Grading will be similar in these sections as well.

While there will be a divergence in the English courses selected by students starting in grade 10, all the students will receive instruction in grammar, writing skills, and basic literary concepts. In addition, teachers will provide group instruction in the language mechanics skills identified as at less than 50% mastery on the California Test of Basic Skills.

The small number of grade 10 students, including the EEN, who were identified as being significantly below the expected norm will receive individual assistance in the identified areas of need. (Significantly below means that the student has scored in the bottom 10% of his or her norm group.)

Monitoring Progress

The grade 10 teacher advisors will meet for 15 minutes daily with their advisees as a group, and part of this time will be used for goal setting in English and other courses.

The grade 10 teacher advisor will meet with each of his or her advisees in at least six individual conferences per year. Parents will participate in two of the conferences, one at the end of the first quarter and one at the end of the third. English progress will be discussed in these conferences, as will the other academic areas.

All implementers as a group will meet for one hour on each eighth school day and will use part of the time to discuss student progress in English and to resolve any problems associated with the English classes.

Comment: Implementation activities differ greatly according to the improvement project. However, four important considerations pertaining to any project are that (a) the roles and responsibilities of the task force members and the implementers are clear with respect to both implementation and monitoring; (b) time, space, materials, and other physical arrangements are worked out so that the implementers can function with maximum effectiveness; (c) the implementers are supported by the task force and the district office; and (d) each implementer receives immediate assistance when a problem is experienced.

Effective implementation often calls for more time and effort than was anticipated. When this occurs, a cutback in activities, an extension of time, or additional incentives to the implementers may be in order. In any event, the problem must be resolved or the implementation cannot be continued successfully.

The purposes of monitoring are to ensure that the improvement activities are proceeding smoothly and that progress toward goal attainment is being made. Accordingly, monitoring starts early and continues at regular intervals throughout the year.

The monitor employs many different techniques to gain information, such as observation, interviewing, conferring, and examining records. An equally great variety of techniques is used to confirm successful implementation, to identify problems and concerns, and to assist the implementers.

Monitoring of progress toward goal attainment is carried out by teachers, teacher advisors, or counselors when students are the beneficiaries of the project. In addition, a person other than the implementers always participates in the monitoring process, regardless of whether or not the goal pertains to student outcomes.

This is necessary for monitoring the implementation of the improvement activities, rather than student progress alone. Not providing for adequate monitoring when planning the project risks failure. Implementers don't respond well to unplanned monitoring.

9. Evaluation in Terms of Goal Attainment and Effectiveness of Activities

Normal Curve Equivalents (NCE) on the Comprehensive Tests of Basic Skills subtests of Reading (Vocabulary and Comprehension), Spelling, and Language (Mechanics and Expression) will be obtained for all grade 10 students in the spring of 1984. These results will be compared with the NCEs from the spring of 1983 for the same students to determine (a) whether each student has maintained high achievement and raised low achievement, and (b) whether the high mean subscores of grade 9 have been maintained in grade 10 and whether the low mean scores have been raised.

The EIC and the implementers will use the preceding results in assessing the effectiveness of the grade 10 English program of instruction, the advising process, the monitoring process, and the testing program.

Comment: The purposes of evaluating toward the end of each year are to ascertain the extent to which goals were attained, to determine the effectiveness of the improvement activities, and to provide a data base for identifying areas of improvement for the ensuing year. The purpose here, as for monitoring progress, is not to arrive at judgments that may influence the salary or job security of the teachers, counselors, principals, or district officials. A written statement is needed from the school board indicating that the results of the evaluation will be used for the three improvement purposes and that they will not be used to evaluate personnel.

10. Refinement

The degree of goal attainment will be shared with the entire faculty through the EIC. Whether this specific improvement project for grade 10 will be continued during the 1984-85 school year is dependent upon the student outcomes. However, the cycle of goal-setting, implementation, and evaluation in English for one or more grades will be continued on an annual basis through the EIC and through the process of formulating an Annual School Improvement Plan.

Comment: Three or more years are required to institutionalize a comprehensive improvement project, and refinement continues thereafter or the improved practices grow stagnant. This idea is incorporated in the annual plan, thereby ensuring awareness on the part of the whole staff, parents, school board members, and the public in general.

School staffs experience renewal as they attain important goals, acquire new knowledge, increase their competencies, and receive recognition for their successes. However, the recognition as well as the means of gaining new knowledge and increasing competence are not always built into an improvement plan. In turn, entire staffs experience "burnout." To ensure renewal and to avoid burnout, schools now give attention to staff renewal, not only as part of their improvement planning but also as an integral element of refining their self-improvement capability. In some schools, the EIC assumes this initiative; in other schools a renewal task force is established. It implements the basic assessment-goal setting-planning-implementation-monitoring-evaluation strategy in fostering continual self-renewal.

11. Time Schedule

	Starting Date	Ending Date
Preplanning	October 1981	June 1982
Planning	September 1982	June 1983
Preparatory Activities	March 1983	August 1983
First-Year Implementation	August 1983	June 1984
Refinement/Renewal	June 1984	Ongoing

Comment: A good time schedule includes dates, often to the nearest month, for starting and ending each phase of the basic improvement strategy. The scheduled dates are not a contract to be enforced but estimates of when activities should commence and be completed in order to attain the goals that are set. In most projects, there is some overlapping of the planning, preparatory, and implementation activities.

12. Budget

	Planning and Preparation	First-Year Implementation/ Evaluation	Second-Year Refinement/ Renewal
Substitute teachers	$700.00	$700.00	$350.00
Summer employment			
Consultants		$300.00	$300.00

(continued)

18

	Planning and Preparation	First-Year Implementation/ Evaluation	Second-Year Refinement/ Renewal
Workshops, seminars etc.	$300.00		
Materials, tests etc.			
Travel	$250.00	$250.00	$250.00
Other			

Comment: A budget for each project is prepared by the EIC or a task force. The most critical items to consider are given above. Starting even the smallest project typically calls for additional funds. A budget estimate for the first and second years of _refinement_ is made to ensure that a project does not get dropped or curtailed for lack of essential funding. In general, staff time, not included above, is secured to carry out improvement projects by dropping less critical maintenance tasks.

Providing Internal and External Support

The primary sources of monetary support for improvement projects is the district. The best way to ensure that money is available for improvement projects is to have a separate budget item for improvement that is in addition to the regular budget allocation for each school.

The principal and the district office support each school's improvement program in addition to providing money. They verbally support each project to the school board, parents, and the school's educational community. Cooperatively and interactively, the principal and the district office take steps to ensure that the members of the EIC, members of each task force, and implementers with mutual improvement interests have a common time each week during regularly scheduled hours to confer, plan, and carry out other essential inservice/staff development activities. Similarly, the principal and the district office take initiative for securing the support and participation of parents and other community individuals and groups.

The large majority of local schools, district offices, and school boards have monetary and other resources for establishing and maintaining a districtwide improvement capability, given an adequate level of monetary support from the state. However, intellectual and technical support are regularly provided to the local school from external sources in order to continually provide more schooling to students and higher quality schooling. The external groups include the state education agency, intermediate agencies, teacher education agencies, and professional education associations.

In addition to a fixed level of monetary support, the state education agency takes initiative for activities such as:

Stimulating the school improvement activities of local schools through policies and standards.

Providing additional financial support to local schools for comprehensive improvement projects and also for high-risk exploratory projects.

Providing for teachers' job descriptions to be changed, if necessary, to enable them to participate in student advisement and in leading improvement projects.

Developing new certification standards as necessary to meet changing societal conditions and related demands on education.

Teacher education institutions, working cooperatively with local schools and the state education agency, take initiative for activities such as:

Evaluating their programs to prepare administrators, counselors, teachers, and other educational personnel; revising existing programs; and developing new programs to meet changing societal conditions and related demands on education.

Developing and offering credit courses and noncredit arrangements tailored to local schools' improvement programs that enable teachers and others to engage in the school's improvement activities more effectively.

Arranging with local schools for cooperative preparation of student teachers and interns.

Professional education associations at the local, state, and national levels take initiative for activities such as:

Providing leadership to their members in educational improvement.

Identifying and publicizing local schools that demonstrate improved schooling practices and outcomes.

Working out contract provisions that facilitate the role of the teacher in school improvement.

Formulating District Guidelines

We saw earlier that the main source of improvement support to local schools is the district office. We also observed that a district improvement committee, interacting with the local school staff, prepares the district's improvement guidelines. The nature of the committee's work may be inferred from the completed guidelines that follow. I have entered comments after some of the items to clarify the development of guidelines.

District Guidelines for
Annual School Improvement Planning, 1984-85:
Cedarburg School District, Cedarburg, WI

The Cedarburg School District guidelines for preparing the Annual School Improvement Plan were designed as a policy vehicle to insure that the School District is addressing areas wherein improvement can be realized while also maintaining areas where outcomes have proven to be satisfactory. The attached Annual School Improvement Plan contains the rationale, the goals, the areas of improvement, the organizational procedures, the assessment process, and the timelines which need to be followed.

School districts and individual school buildings can considerably improve their services when the goals of the district and the Board of Education are clearly delineated and clarified for the building principal and the professional staff. Local research data designed to measure student outcomes in the cognitive, psychomotor, health, and affective domains are a valuable resource for determining a school district's effectiveness and monitoring school improvement progress.

Further information about specific Cedarburg School District and school building improvement plans can be obtained by contacting the Cedarburg School District.

Dr. Herbert J. Klausmeier of the Wisconsin Center for Education Research served as a consultant to the District in developing the District Guidelines. He can be contacted at the University of Wisconsin in Madison regarding both local school and district level improvement planning.

Frank M. Kennedy, Superintendent
CEDARBURG SCHOOL DISTRICT
W68 N611 Evergreen Boulevard
Cedarburg, Wisconsin 53012
414-377-6030
August 1984, Revised March 1985

District Guidelines for Preparing
Annual School Improvement Plan

I. Rationale

The major educational goal of the Cedarburg School District is to provide each child attending the Cedarburg public schools an effective educational program. To attain this goal, consistent and continuous effort is required by personnel of each school, the District Office, and the Board of Education. Accordingly, District guidelines are needed to assure that each school, the District Office, and the Board of Education establish and maintain a permanent improvement capability regardless of any changes that may occur in key personnel of a school, the District Office, the Board of Education, or the state education agency.

It is imperative that we of the Cedarburg School District take the initiative for improvement rather than merely responding to directives of federal education agencies, the state education agency, or other organizations. We know the educational needs of our community, and only we can provide the essential instructional, advisement, administrative, and other services to the students. We recognize the value of external stimulation and the need for continuing monetary support from the state education agency and federal agencies. We in this District, however, must decide whether and how to implement any proposals for improvement, and only we are directly responsible to the students and their parents as well as to the taxpayers of this District.

II. Goals

The outcome of establishing a permanent improvement capability, both in the district and within each school, is the continuous improvement of education locally. This involves the improvement of areas of weakness and the maintenance of areas of strength. This goal incorporates efforts to coordinate education by the schools, keeping in mind the general direction of the District at large.

III. Broad Areas of Improvement

The Cedarburg schools are operated for the purpose of providing high quality education to the students of the District, as is reflected in the philosophy and program goals of the Cedarburg School District. Accordingly, the broad areas of improvement will be related first and foremost to student outcomes of schooling (a) in the cognitive domain (attainment of knowledge, problem-solving skills, learning strategies, thinking skills, creativity, etc., mainly in the academic fields); (b) in the psychomotor and health domain (attainment of information, skills, strategies, creativity, etc. pertaining to physical/psychomotor activities and health); and (c) in the affective domain (development of favorable attitudes toward learning, schooling, peers, etc. and of positive self-concepts in the academic and nonacademic areas).

Regular attendance, punctuality, good conduct, avoidance of the use of alcohol and other drugs, and continuation in school through high school graduation are other desired student outcomes.

As a means of maintaining already satisfactory student outcomes and raising those less than satisfactory, the District or a school will focus on the broad areas of improvement of the curriculum, evaluation, advisement, instruction, planning, inservice, etc. Educational innovations and/or materials by themselves are not to be considered as broad areas of improvement. Although student outcomes will be the foremost area of improvement, attitudes of and participation by parents and other citizens in the District educative processes, teacher punctuality and attendance, principal leadership, staff morale, and job satisfaction may be included as broad areas of improvement inasmuch as they markedly influence attainment of desired student outcomes.

IV. District Improvement Committee

Membership: Superintendent, Director of Instruction, a principal from each of the three instructional levels (K-5, 6-8, 9-12), and one member of the Board of Education. This committee is responsible for planning and making decisions regarding both the District and local school improvement programs. At the District level, the committee establishes the annual District list of broad areas of improvement from lists submitted by the local schools and identifies the priority or central theme for all schools in the District. At the local school level, this committee reviews local school improvement plans for approval, disapproval, or modification and monitors their progress throughout the year.

23

V. District Leadership

The Superintendent has overall responsibility for all improvement activities. The District's Director of Instruction, working with the District Improvement Committee, has responsibility for preparing the annual District improvement plan and evaluating and reporting its results yearly.

VI. The District's Annual Improvement Plan

The first step in developing the District annual improvement plan is establishing a list of broad areas of improvement. The procedure for this begins in each individual school building in the fall as a function of the School Improvement Committee (or similar group) in that building and its annual assessment of student outcomes (see XI). The ideas generated at the school level are discussed by the Administrative Council and forwarded to the District Improvement Committee.

The District Improvement Committee reviews the broad areas received from the Administrative Council and selects a central theme for District-wide improvement. It also issues a prioritized list of broad areas of suggested improvement for local school improvement plans.

The District Improvement Committee then issues a goal statement for the District improvement plan and suggests areas for improvement in each school. The goal statement will be specific enough to allow each school to prepare a detailed plan and general enough to allow each school the flexibility to meet unique building needs.

Schools then submit a preliminary outline of their local school plan relating to the District theme. The District Improvement Committee reviews local school outlines and approves, disapproves, or modifies them as needed. Schools are then free to develop their outline into a final improvement plan.

The District improvement plan emerges after individual plans have been developed and approved. The District plan will describe the common District-wide improvement programs and will include descriptions of program/staff support for local school plans, budget support for the District-wide project and local school plans, a monitoring plan for both the District-wide project and specific school improvement plans, and dates for reports, both interim and final. In brief, the District plan will describe central support to the schools in their individual efforts as well as the plan for any given long-term central theme for District-wide improvement. (Format for District and school plans presented in XII.)

24

VII. Local School Improvement Committee

The local school organizational arrangements for formulating each school's annual improvement plan will be an inhouse committee chaired by the principal and consisting of a representative group of teachers, chosen either by team or by department. This committee will be responsible for conducting the school's annual assessment procedures and for formulating a local improvement plan. It will also be responsible for developing a plan at the school level for meeting the District-wide improvement project goals.

VIII. Local School Leadership

The principal in each school will be responsible for preparing the school improvement plan for the ensuing year and the report of results for the current year. The local School Improvement Committee will provide input and assessment in preparing the local school improvement plan. Decisions of this committee will be based on discussions with the staff so that all will have the opportunity for input.

IX. Local School Annual Improvement Plan

Each school is responsible for developing two types of improvement plans.

One plan describes what the local school will do to meet the goal of the District-wide improvement plan.

The second plan will generally reflect the needs of the local school with reference to the District's annual list of broad areas of improvement. This planning begins as the school starts to collect its data. The principal and the School Improvement Committee analyze the data to identify areas of improvement unique to the local building.

If the local School Improvement Committee wishes to consider an area for improvement not on the District's annual list of broad areas of improvement, it needs prior approval from the District Improvement Committee before this second plan can be undertaken.

All local school improvement plans will be forwarded by the principals to the District Improvement Committee for approval. In general, all annual local school improvement plans will be approved by the District Improvement Committee as long as evidence exists that there is a need for improvement, the plan supports the District philosophy, and the plan is not merely a new innovation in education. All school improvement plans will be monitored at least twice during the year by the local school improvement committee and reports forwarded to the District Improvement Committee.

X. District Support

The District will provide monetary support for long-term projects of merit. Such monetary support will be included in the District's annual spring budget process but will be separate from the local school budget. Program support is available in terms of evaluation design, additional data gathering, and other general assistance as possible.

The District will also undertake, in addition to the required semiannual monitoring reports to be made by principals, onsite monitoring efforts to be conducted as needed by the Superintendent of Schools, the Director of Instruction, and other members of the District Improvement Committee.

XI. Annual Assessment Process

An integral part of the development of both District and local school improvement plans is the assessment process. Annually, all schools will examine student outcomes in the areas of achievement and ability.

In assessing student achievement, schools are encouraged to examine standardized achievement test results, criterion-referenced test results, locally constructed CRT results, PBE results, grade point averages, student grade reports, teacher observations, samples of student work, scholastic competitive results, and other indirect measures.

Normative test results are considered primary indicators. The District normative and criterion-referenced tests relate to reading, math, language arts, science, and social studies. It is important that results in all areas of the curriculum (including the fine and applied arts) be examined.

In assessing student attitudes, schools are encouraged to examine the results of such formal and informal measures as attendance records; discipline and suspension records; dropout rate; post-high school survey; incidence of vandalism; teacher observations; student, teacher, and parent surveys; and other measures of school climate.

Parent and community perceptions of student achievement and attitude can also be useful in the assessment process. Parent and community involvement in the school are indicators to be considered in the assessment process.

Once the collecting and analyzing of data has been completed, the first step in the annual assessment process is the identification of areas of possible improvement or maintenance. Next the possible areas are prioritized. Finally, areas for improvement are selected from the list of priorities. In general, high priority should be attached to areas where student outcomes are lowest and where the most effort is needed to improve and maintain high levels of achievement.

XII. Improvement Plan Format

Both the final District plan and final school improvement plans will utilize the following format:

1. Area of Improvement
2. Need or Rationale
3. Percent of Students and Grades Involved
4. Persons Who Will Plan, Coordinate, and Evaluate the Program
5. Persons Who Will Implement the Program
6. Improvement Goals (General and Performance)
7. Preparatory Activities
8. First-year Implementation Activities and Monitoring Progress
9. Evaluation in Terms of Goal Attainment and Effectiveness of Activities
10. Refinement and Renewal
11. Time Schedule
12. Budget

Comment: We observe that each school generates a plan related to its perceived unique needs, and it also recommends one or more districtwide goals/priorities to the District Improvement Committee. The district office synthesizes recommendations of its various committees and also presents one or more goals/priorities to the District Improvement Committee. Based on this input, the committee identifies at least one districtwide priority that each school addresses in its annual plan. This approach is highly recommended in that it provides each school a maximum amount of autonomy yet no school proceeds as an island unto itself, unmindful of the larger ecological system of which it is a part.

27

TIME LINE FOR DISTRICT AND LOCAL SCHOOL IMPROVEMENT PLANNING

SEPT 1 —— OCT 1 —— DEC 1 —— DEC 15 —— JAN 15 —— FEB 15 —— MAR 1 —— MAR 15 —— APR 1 —— MAY 1 —— MAY 15 —— JUL 30

DISTRICT PLANNING FOR NEXT YEAR

LOCAL SCHOOL PLANNING

Above the timeline (District planning):

- **OCT 1** — District improvement plan established for current year

- **DEC 1** — Local School Improvement Committees submit to DIC suggested areas for District-wide improvement

- **DEC 15** — Principals submit list of possible areas of improvement to Administrative Council

- **JAN 15** — DIC establishes areas of improvement and theme for common priorities

- **FEB 15** — DIC issues goal statement for District improvement project

- **MAR 1** — Improvement budget set (estimate)

- **MAR 15** — Schools submit to DIC for review preliminary outline of local school plan related to District improvement project

- **MAY 1** — Schools submit final local school improvement plans for meeting District improvement project

- **MAY 15** — DIC approves schools' plans for meeting District Improvement project and finalizes budget

Below the timeline (Local school planning):

- **SEPT 1** — Schools formulate local schools' local school improvement plans: for current year

- **OCT 1** — *Final local schools' improvement plans approved by DIC: for current year

- **JAN 15** — Interim progress report due: for current year

- **MAR 1** — Improvement budget set for following year (estimate)

- **APR 1** — Interim progress report due: for current year

- **MAY 1** — Begin to collect and analyze current year's data

- **MAY 15** — Outlines of topics not on DIC list of approved areas of improvement presented at this time

- **JUL 30** — Final report due: for current year

* Local school improvement plans and outlines may be submitted to District Improvement Committee anytime after data have been collected and analyzed but before October 1 for local school improvement plan that is unique to that school and before May 1 for local school improvement plan that meets district improvement project.

28

Chapter 2
Administering School Improvement: Dynamic Leadership

Rationale

Design Objectives

Preplanning Activities

**Local School Administrative-Organizational
Structures and Processes**

**School Improvement Committee
Composition and Functioning, 1984-85:
Steuben Middle School, Milwaukee, WI**

**District Administrative-Organizational
Structures and Processes**

**District Improvement Committee
Composition and Functioning, 1984-85:
Cedarburg School District, Cedarburg, WI**

**District School Effectiveness Committee
Composition and Functioning, 1984-85:
Milwaukee School District, Milwaukee, WI**

Rationale

The district administrator is responsible for leading the development and institutionalization of a districtwide school improvement program. The building principal has the same responsibility for the school's improvement program. When starting and institutionalizing their improvement programs, district administrators and principals demonstrate three kinds of leadership: assertive, participative, and supportive/facilitative. While the direction is typically from assertive to supportive/facilitative, all three forms of leadership are relevant at specific times in particular situations. These forms of leadership are illustrated by activities of the district administrator.

Assertive leadership on the part of the district administrator implies that districtwide improvement activities are planned and get started and completed in a timely manner. Assertive leadership does not imply the means by which the leader accomplishes this. However, the district administrator properly makes public his or her desire for each school of the district to develop a self-improvement capability. School board support of this decision is secured. The district administrator then forms the district improvement committee.

The district administrator shares leadership responsibility hereafter as the committee members participate in all the decisions about how each school will proceed and what the district will do to support each school. These and other ideas are put into district guidelines.

The district administrator and other district officials support the principals and their staffs in implementing the guidelines from the outset. Moreover, the district monitors each school's progress to insure that district assistance is forthcoming as needed.

The principal leads a school staff in a manner similar to the district administrator leading the principals of the district. The principal communicates his commitment to the idea of developing a self-improvement capability, organizes the school's improvement committee, chairs the committee meetings, sets the early agenda, and participates with the members in making decisions about how the staff will proceed. The principal supports the committee members in implementing the decisions of the committee and facilitates each teacher's implementation of the improvement activities.

The principal develops leadership among the staff by transferring leadership responsibilities as rapidly as possible, first to the members of the committee and then to other members of the staff. For example, high school department chairs and middle school team leaders develop improvement plans, monitor progress, and evaluate the results. The principal not only supports the staff in these efforts, he or she aids the staff in carrying out their improvement activities.

Principals and district administrators who proceed in this manner achieve remarkable success over a period of a few years. Each school makes progress toward institutionalizing its self-improvement capability as it maintains already satisfactory student outcomes from year to year and betters those not satisfactory.

On the other hand, when school improvement is a volunteer activity of an occasional interested principal and when the district administrator shies away from districtwide leadership, schooling continues to deteriorate on a districtwide basis. The occasional volunteer principal and school staff soon recognize that there is no payoff for creative effort and hard work, except as it may be recognized by the students and parents. This, however, is not a sufficient basis for institutionalizing a self-improvement capability. Without district support, the school's improvement capability is lost when the principal leaves or when essential monetary and technical support are withdrawn as other spur-of-the-moment panaceas receive higher priority in the district.

This chapter gives the objectives for establishing district office and local school administrative-organizational arrangements and then indicates the preparatory activities and the detailed procedures for starting the local school and the district office arrangements. The arrangements of Steuben Middle School, the Cedarburg School District, and the Milwaukee School District are presented to illustrate exemplary local school and district structures and processes.

Design Objectives

Comprehensive Objective

The administrative arrangements of the central office and each school provide for cooperative planning and shared decision making by the persons responsible for implementing the plans and decisions that are made, mainly district officials, principals, teachers, and counselors.

Illustrative District Office Enabling Objectives

A district School Improvement Committee consisting of the district administrator and representative elementary, middle, and high school principals, and possibly teachers, counselors, and school board members:

> Develops guidelines for establishing and maintaining a self-improvement capability in each school and in the district office.

> Leads and coordinates the districtwide implementation of the guidelines.

Illustrative Local School Enabling Objectives

> An Educational Improvement Committee (or other committee or council) that has representatives of the administrative team, curriculum coordinators, counselors, and teachers leads and coordinates the school's educational improvement activities with input from the total faculty. Students, parents, and other citizens participate in meetings of the Educational Improvement Committee when matters of concern to them are on the agenda, and they may serve as members of the Committee.

> The principal provides leadership and, with appropriate involvement of members of the Educational Improvement Committee and the school staff:

> > Establishes policies and procedures that facilitate the functioning of the school's Educational Improvement Committee.

> > Coordinates the use of facilities, materials, equipment, supplies, and other resources.

> > Arranges teachers' class schedules and provides time, space, and other physical arrangements that are needed for the Educational Improvement Committee, teaching teams, and other mutual-interest groups to plan and carry out their work.

> > Establishes effective two-way communication among administrators, other staff, teachers, and students; and between the school and parents and citizens of the community.

> > Participates as a member of the district School Improvement Committee.

Transmits information to and from the district committee.

Attempts to have implemented the decisions made by the district committee.

Preplanning Activities

The district administrator, other district officials, and principals:

Gain a complete understanding of district-local school structures and processes, improvement strategies, facilitative school components, and support arrangements.

View and discuss the filmstrip "Administrative Arrangements for Shared Decision Making in Secondary Schools."

Listen to and discuss relevant sections of the audiocassette "Experiences of a Middle School and Two Senior High Schools with Administrative Arrangements for Shared Decision Making."

Read textbook Chapter 8, "Administrative Arrangements and Processes."

Gain an overview of the goal-based improvement strategy and the two primary strategies by viewing the three filmstrips describing these strategies and surveying Chapters 2, 3, and 7 of the textbook and Chapters 3 and 4 of this Guide.

Gain an overview of the facilitative components and support arrangements by viewing the other six filmstrips and surveying all other chapters of the textbook and this Guide.

Visit schools and district offices that have developed and institutionalized a self-improvement capability and secure completed plans and guidelines of similar-sized schools and districts.

The district improvement committee, with input to and from each school, prepares the district guidelines.

Local School Administrative-Organizational Structures and Processes

When there are district guidelines, the principal follows them in developing a self-improvement capability in his or her school. However, principals are urged to start an improvement capability in the absence of guidelines. Without guidelines the principal takes more initiative but secures district office and possibly school board support at the start. Moreover, the principal communicates regularly with the district office to insure continuing approval and support.

After securing district commitment, the principal organizes the school's improvement committee or allocates school improvement to an existing group or groups. The number of committee members and their selection varies according to the size and level of schooling.

In the senior high school organized into either separate subject departments or broad field areas, the teacher representatives on the committee include part or all of the chairpersons, or they may be elected, volunteers, or principal-selected teachers from part or all of the departments or areas. In the middle school and the junior high school organized as the senior high school, the teachers are represented in the same way as in the senior high school. In middle schools and junior high schools in which the teachers are organized into academic teams and other special teams, a representative teacher is elected by, or volunteers from, each team. In elementary schools in which the teachers are organized into teams, a teacher from each team is elected or volunteers. In elementary schools organized by grades, a representative teacher from each grade is elected or volunteers. In school districts in which there is more than one high school or middle/junior high school, membership on the school's improvement committee is greatly facilitated by district guidelines that indicate either a preferred method or alternative means of securing the teacher representation.

In most schools, the principal chairs the meetings of the improvement committee; however, in some schools, a teacher or other person is elected. Regardless of how the meetings are conducted, the improvement committee takes initiative for implementing the following improvement processes:

Makes the staff aware of the need for establishing a self-improvement capability and builds staff commitment.

Uses available assessment information and gathers more, if necessary, to ascertain the extent to which the school's educational goals are being attained, and identifies and prioritizes areas of improvement annually.

Develops an improvement plan for each selected area of improvement annually.

Ensures that the relevant staff is properly prepared to implement the planned activities before starting the implementation.

Implements the planned activities and monitors progress.

Evaluates the effectiveness of the improvement activities annually and reports the results of the evaluation annually.

Repeats the cycle annually, starting with Phase 2, in refining the improved practices.

Some principals find it appropriate to form a task force on administrative arrangements. They do this to insure that the teachers and the principal clarify their roles and responsibilities with respect to the preceding improvement process and with respect to developing their planning skills and small-group interaction skills. In schools in which neither the principal nor the teachers have carried out the preceding process, a considerable amount of preparatory activity is required.

As a preparation aid three simulations are available from the Wisconsin Center for Education Research: one set for elementary school, another for middle school, and one for high school. The simulations are designed to aid a committee identify possible broad areas of improvement, clarify individual committee members' roles and responsibilities, and use test information in prioritizing improvement projects. The simulations are also designed to encourage open communication among committee members and to enable them to ascertain the extent to which they agree regarding critical issues related to school improvement.

School Improvement Committee
Composition and Functioning, 1984-85:
Steuben Middle School, Milwaukee, WI

Steuben Middle School enrolled 850 students in grades 7 and 8 in 1984-85. Its School Coordinating Committee includes the principal, one learning coordinator, 12 teachers, one paraprofessional, and one teacher union representative. Each teacher represents the members of the academic team, fine arts and vocational education

36

team, or exceptional education team to which he or she belongs. The paraprofessional is selected by all paraprofessionals assigned to the building. The committee meets weekly for 45 to 60 minutes.

The Steuben School Coordinating Committee is responsible for the development, monitoring, and evaluation of an annual school effectiveness plan. The first plan was developed in the spring of 1982. Periodically throughout the school year, each segment of the current year's plan is reviewed by the School Coordinating Committee to insure that the listed goals are being worked on. At the same time, the degree of success in reaching the goal is evaluated by examining available data or determining if the activities stated in the individual goals are being conducted. At these times, specific goals may be identified for special attention during the remainder of the school year. During April and May, the Committee evaluates the entire plan for the ending school year and determines what additions, changes, or deletions will be made for the next school year.

Comment: The composition and functioning of Steuben's School Coordinating Committee are similar to those of the other 17 middle schools of Milwaukee. All of the middle school staffs are organized into three kinds of teams: academic, exceptional education, and fine arts and vocational education.

Before proceeding, we should recognize that in schools of other districts the improvement committees meet less often but for a longer time period, especially when developing the plan for the ensuing year.

District Administrative-Organizational Structures and Processes

The district administrator working with the schools, school board, and community takes initiative for establishing and maintaining a self-improvement capability in the district office and in each school. The district administrator designates a district office person to take primary responsibility for the implementation and monitoring of the district office and districtwide improvement activities. In turn, a district improvement committee consisting of district officials and representative principals, and in some districts teachers and school board members, is formed. This committee takes initiative for formulating the district guidelines that provide the essential information used by each school in developing an annual improvement plan. A set of guidelines follows later. Before turning to them, we may consider other interest areas of the district committee related to the various improvement strategies and facilitative schooling components given earlier in Figure 1.1 of Chapter 1.

Goal-Based Strategy

A considerable amount of staff time is required to implement this strategy, and principals and teachers on the improvement committee need assistance in learning to develop an improvement plan, monitor progress, and evaluate the results. Accordingly, districtwide procedures are worked out that

Eliminate school and district committees that are not directed toward bringing about measurable improvements from year to year.

Insure that teachers' class schedules are arranged so that the district committee and each school committee can meet weekly for at least two hours.

Provide the preparatory (inservice/staff development) activities needed by the committee to learn to implement the strategy.

For each other strategy and facilitative school component given earlier in Figure 1.1, only the comprehensive objective follows. These comprehensive objectives appear in later chapters of this Guide along with illustrative enabling objectives. In each later chapter these comprehensive and enabling objectives of the design are followed with detailed implementation suggestions.

Individual Educational Programming Strategy

An educational program of course work and other activities is arranged for each student each semester that satisfies his or her developmental needs and characteristics and also meets district and state requirements.

Individual Instructional Programming Strategy

An instructional program that takes into account the student's aptitudes, interests, motivation, learning styles, career goals, and other personal and social characteristics is arranged for each student in each course and other activity that is part of the student's total educational program.

Curriculum

The school's curriculum is based on the district's educational philosophy and the school's program goals. Course goals and course

38

content and instruction are in accord with the district philosophy and the program goals. The school's curriculum is structured to meet state and district requirements, but it is adapted by the school and individual teachers to take into account the differing educational needs of students.

Student Decision Making, Self-Discipline, and Citizenship

Students progressively assume more responsibility for learning well, self-disciplined conduct, and good citizenship.

Evaluating Student Learning and Educational Programs

A districtwide program of testing and other data gathering is maintained to ascertain the extent to which the school's program goals and the district's goals are attained annually. The individual student's progress toward attaining his or her course objectives, the student's instructional program in each course, the student's total educational program, and the school's total educational program are evaluated systematically; and the results of the evaluation are used in improving the educative processes of the school. (Evaluation is interpreted to include pre-assessment, ongoing assessment, and post-assessment.)

Organization for Instruction

The faculty and students are organized into small groups that permit the instructional programming strategy to be implemented effectively.

Organization for Advising

The faculty and students are organized into small groups that permit advising to be personalized and the educational programming strategy to be implemented effectively.

Home-School-Community Relations

Effective communication and cooperative educational efforts between the school and the community are carried out as part of a program of home-school-community relations.

Internal and External Support

The environment for learning and instruction in the school and for work and other experiences in the community is enriched through the technical and material support provided by the school and district and by external agencies, such as the state education agency, intermediate education agencies, teacher education institutions, and professional education associations. (Support was discussed in Chapter 1.)

District Improvement Committee
Composition and Functioning, 1984-85:
Cedarburg School District, Cedarburg, WI

The Cedarburg School District has three elementary schools with a total enrollment of 877, one middle school with an enrollment of 603, and one high school with an enrollment of 1,118.

The Director of Instruction and Special Services leads the districtwide improvement activities on a day-to-day basis.

The District Improvement Committee (DIC) includes the superintendent of schools, director of instruction (chairperson), the high school principal, the middle school principal, one elementary school principal, and one school board member. The superintendent, director of instruction, high school principal, and middle school principal are one-of-a-kind positions. The elementary school principal is appointed by the superintendent of schools; and the school board member, who is appointed by the Board of Education president, is also chairperson of the Board Curriculum Committee. The committee does not meet on a predetermined schedule. Six half-day meetings were scheduled in 1984-85.

The committee spends considerable time reacting to the plans of each school. The chair of the committee spent a morning at one school with the school's improvement committee in clarifying and planning. Monitoring activities have been undertaken by the committee in two ways: visitations to schools and discussion of the schools' end-of-semester interim progress reports. In one case, the chair of the committee spent another morning discussing how much progress a school had actually made through January. It is expected that the committee will spend much of its time discussing each school's evaluation of this year's projects. This topic is scheduled for early June.

The district officials consist of the Superintendent, the Business Manager, and the Director of Instruction and Special Services. The amount of time available to aid each school is very limited. The Director of Instruction spends most of his available time assisting one or two schools with planning (actually helping to write the plan in detail in one case) and very little time participating in the implementation per se. The Director of Instruction also monitors each school's progress on a very limited basis as part of his other duties with the schools. He will spend a considerable amount of time on the evaluation and in determining the schools' needs for renewal activities.

40

The Superintendent has not been directly involved in planning or implementing, has participated in monitoring, and will be involved in the evaluation. The Business Manager has not participated with the exception of setting improvement budgets as directed by the committee (DIC).

Comment: Since there are only three district officials, much responsibility is placed on each principal for developing the school's self-improvement capability. We might assume that all five principals would have taken this initiative voluntarily. However, five years after the first one had, two were just starting while one was still strongly resisting the idea. This school did not develop an annual improvement plan until the district guidelines, presented earlier in Chapter 1, were formulated and endorsed by the school board.

District School Effectiveness Committee Composition and Functioning, 1984-85: Milwaukee School District, Milwaukee, WI

The Milwaukee School District has 100 K-6 elementary schools with a total enrollment of 57,000, 18 grade 7-8 middle schools with a total enrollment of 10,000, and 15 grade 9-12 high schools with a total enrollment of 22,500.

The School Effectiveness Coordinator, who is also a district curriculum specialist, leads the districtwide improvement activities on a day-to-day basis. This leadership is only part of his duties; he continues other duties as a curriculum specialist.

The District School Effectiveness Planning Committee consists of the Deputy Superintendent, the Assistant Superintendent for Curriculum and Instruction, the Assistant Superintendent for School Services, the three Administrative Specialists for Elementary Schools, the Administrative Specialist for Middle Schools, the Administrative Specialist for High Schools, the Coordinator of Educational Research, the Director of the Staff Development Academy, nine elementary school principals, two middle school principals, one high school principal, the Coordinator of the Secondary School Effectiveness Program, one Middle School Curriculum Specialist, and one Secondary School Curriculum Specialist.

These persons are identified in the District Guidelines by their positions.

This committee annually evaluates and establishes systemwide school effectiveness goals and communicates these goals throughout the district, develops the annual district plan for school effectiveness, reviews and evaluates the current year's district plan, receives and reacts to the plans of all schools, and reviews and evaluates the plans of selected schools in individual conferences with the principals. The committee meets four times during the school year.

The **District School Effectiveness Advisory Committee** includes the three Elementary School Curriculum Specialists, the Middle School Curriculum Specialist, the High School Curriculum Specialist, the Deputy Superintendent, and a representative from the Division of Curriculum and Instruction, the Division of Human Resources, the Division of Exceptional Education and Supportive Services, the Division of Planning and Long-Range Development, and the Business Department. In addition, representatives are appointed by the Deputy Superintendent from elementary, middle, and high schools to include one principal, a parent, and a teacher from one school of each level. This Committee is chaired by the Deputy Superintendent who is responsible for convening the meetings. The Committee serves as a reaction group to district plans for school effectiveness, provides advice regarding future plans, and communicates district plans to the groups represented by the committee members. The Committee has one scheduled meeting each year and may meet more often.

District office personnel aid the schools in planning, implementing, monitoring, and evaluating their school's effectiveness activities as follows:

The **Board of School Directors** receives and reviews a yearly report on school effectiveness activities.

The **Superintendent and the Superintendent's Cabinet** make periodic school visits to discuss plan implementation and review selected plans.

The **Deputy Superintendent** chairs the School Effectiveness Planning Committee and convenes an annual meeting of the District School Effectiveness Advisory Committee. In addition, the Deputy Superintendent reviews selected school effectiveness plans.

The **Assistant Superintendent for Curriculum and Instruction** coordinates effective school efforts with other priorities and reviews selected local school plans.

The **Executive Director of Elementary and Secondary Education** supports implementation through the assignment of curriculum specialists and curriculum generalists and their supervisors to the schools.

The Curriculum Specialists examine literature on effective instructional practices for application to their subject areas, analyze subject area data and disseminate it to department chairs, meet with principals regarding effective instructional practices, involve department chairs in analyzing instructional practices, discuss local school plans with department chairs for subject area implications, provide information to department chairs to enable them to contribute to school staff meetings, and assist in monitoring the implementation of the school plan through contact with department chairs.

The Curriculum and Instruction Generalists participate in school committee meetings, participate in school staff meetings, assist principals in examination of data, monitor implementation, participate in planning day-to-day activities, review plan drafts against a checklist, assist in preparing final plans for next year, and participate in review sessions.

The Coordinator of Educational Research and Program Assessment provides student outcome data, grade analysis reports each grading period, and a year-end school-by-school statistical report and a system-wide summary of statistical information. In addition, the director prepares a year-end summary and report to the Board of School Directors.

The Director of the Staff Development Academy develops and publicizes deadlines and schedules for inservice training grants, receives and rates training proposals, advises recipients of training grants, schedules and implements individual school training grants, provides team training in identified schools, and provides suggested school effectiveness planning day activities.

The Assistant Superintendent for School Services coordinates effective school efforts with other priorities and reviews selected local school plans.

The Administrative Specialists conduct school plan reviews and progress sessions with principals and supervisors.

Comment: The Milwaukee School District required all principals to submit their first school effectiveness plans in June of 1982 for the 1982-83 school year. In 1981-82, two half days per month were given to providing inservice education to the principals.

Many principals in the first year were opposed to the idea of planning. By the spring of 1984, most were strongly supportive of it.

Each successive year after 1982–83, the district office received more input regarding the program from the principals and provided more assistance to the schools. Three truly significant changes emerged across the years as the curriculum specialists and curriculum generalists provided assistance to the schools in planning, implementation, and monitoring rather than in monitoring for the district.

The Staff Development Academy provided inservice/staff development activities tailored specifically to the various schools' effectiveness activities.

The School Effectiveness Advisory Committee was formed.

Thus, leadership from the district moved from high assertiveness to supportive/facilitative. Despite this, and very properly, the district's planning guidelines each successive year provided more detailed information to each school regarding the school's responsibilities and procedures and also regarding the district's responsibilities and procedures.

Chapter 3
Arranging Total Educational Programs for Students:
A Helping Hand

Rationale

Design Objectives

Preplanning Activities

Prototypic Plan

**Improvement Plan—Refining the Individual Educational
Programming Strategy, 1984-85:
Webster Transitional School, Cedarburg, WI**

Rationale

Query students in a typical high school. They will tell you that someone assigns them to courses and extracurricular activities without conferring with them individually. No one regularly monitors their progress or discusses the appropriateness of their programs with them.

Query students in a school in which the improvement strategy of individual educational programming is implemented. They will indicate that a teacher advisor or a counselor plans an appropriate educational program of courses and other educational activities with each student prior to or near the beginning of each semester, then monitors the student's progress in each course on a regular basis throughout the semester, and discusses the appropriateness and value of the program for the student toward the end of the semester. They will say that successively better programs are arranged for them from one semester to the next, and that the curriculum is changed to meet their educational needs more effectively. Middle school students will respond in a similar manner.

Both high school and middle school students will indicate that someone really wants them to do well and gives them personal attention. They like school and are doing well academically.

Schools implement the educational programming strategy in a number of ways:

Through a teacher-advisor program.

Through a homeroom program.

Three to five teachers of an academic team implement the strategy with the 75 to 125 students to whom they teach English, mathematics, science, and social studies.

Counselors are sometimes able to implement it.

These different approaches to educational programming are discussed later in Chapter 11. The focus here is on implementing the strategy, not on who implements it. We refer to the implementers as advisors, whether teachers or counselors. We recognize, too, that how well educational programming works depends in part on the school's pattern of instruction and its curriculum. These are discussed in Chapters 4 and 5, respectively.

As is indicated in Chapter 2 of the textbook, individual educational programming is very different for normally developing

47

students than for students with handicapping conditions. The many conferences and the large amount of paper work and reporting required to meet the provisions of PL 94-142 are not included in the present strategy. (See pp. 39-48 of the text for information about the learning characteristics of middle school and high school students and their educational programs.)

Design Objectives

Comprehensive Objective:

An individual educational program of course work and other activities is arranged for each student each semester that satisfies the student's developmental needs and characteristics and that also meets district and state requirements.

Illustrative Enabling Objectives:

Each student's individual educational program which includes all courses and other activities:

Is planned each semester or year by the student and the student's advisor.

Takes into account the student's aptitude for learning different subject matters, interests, motivation, learning styles, career goals, and other personal and social characteristics.

Provides for experiential learning, including work experience in the community, for students who will benefit from it.

Is monitored cooperatively by the student and the student's advisor throughout the semester.

Is changed as necessary during the semester to assure high quality education for the student.

Is evaluated for appropriateness and worthwhileness at the end of each semester.

Preplanning Activities

Either the members of the Educational Improvement Committee or a task force on arranging an appropriate educational program for each student carry out preplanning activities such as the following:

View and discuss the filmstrip "Educational Programming for the Individual Student: Part I."

Listen to and discuss relevant sections of the audiocassette "Experiences of Two Middle Schools and of Two Senior High Schools with Educational Programming for the Individual Student: Part I."

Study the textbook chapters, filmstrips, and audiocassettes on instructional programming, curriculum, evaluation, and teacher-advising.

Visit schools that are implementing individual educational programming, confer with other schools by phone and mail, and secure descriptions and other printed material on individual educational programming.

Assess their school's present situation and identify how individual educational programming will contribute to improving the school's educative processes.

Outline possible means of implementing individual educational programming, determine the inservice education that will be needed and whether it will be conducted by the school staff or secured from an external source, and estimate the costs of planning and implementation.

Gain faculty and parent commitment to implementing individual educational programming.

Prototypic Plan

The members of either the Educational Improvement Committee or a task force on educational programming prepare the plan. Other teachers, parents, students, and other persons are invited to participate in relevant aspects of the planning process. A district official serves as an ad hoc member of the task force or as a consultant to it.

1. Title

    Implementing the Individual Educational Programming Strategy.

2. Need

    A survey performed by the EIC showed that some students are
not being placed in appropriate courses. Also, the progress of
many students is not being monitored so as to avoid unnecessary
failures, and few students' programs are being evaluated. More
suitable educational programs for students, fewer failures, and
higher achievement are desired.

3. Percent of Students and Grades Involved

    100% of the students of each grade.

4. Persons Who Will Coordinate and Evaluate the Implementation of
    the Strategy

    A task force on educational programming consisting of the
principal, a counselor, and six teachers.

5. Persons Who Will Implement the Strategy

    Teachers and/or counselors.

6. Improvement Goals

General Goal

    Each student, and accordingly the composite group of students
of each grade, will have an educational program that is appropriate
for the student in terms of the student's capability for learning
the material of each course, general interests, career goals, and
learning styles.

Performance Goals

    All the courses of each student will be appropriate for
him or her.

    100% of the students of each grade will have appropriate
total educational programs.

General Goal

    Each student in terms of his or her entering achievement level
or his or her capability for learning the particular subject
matter, and thus the composite group of students of each grade,
will achieve high in the academic subjects as measured by the

standardized achievement test battery; locally constructed, criterion-referenced tests in language, mathematics, reading and writing; and teacher grades.

Performance Goals

Each student of each grade will achieve as high as expected in each academic subject as measured by an achievement test battery.

The percentage of students of each grade passing the locally constructed, criterion-referenced test in language, mathematics, reading, and writing will increase by 5% or more.

The grade point average in each academic subject will be 2.9 or higher.

7. Preparatory Activities

Arrange the planning group's teaching schedules and provide substitute teachers so that the planning group can meet at regularly scheduled times during the school day.

Arrange for the planning group to meet outside school hours as necessary to attend workshops and carry out preparatory activities.

Develop a planning form and guidelines for planning, monitoring, and evaluating each student's educational program.

Carry out the preparatory (inservice/staff development activities) of the prospective advisors. (Some of the preplanning activities given earlier are appropriate for the prospective advisors.)

Ensure that the advisor gains competence (and confidence) in (a) matching the student's educational needs and learning characteristics with the available and potentially available offerings and (b) conducting the planning conference and the follow-up conferences with the student and his or her parents.

8. First-Year Implementation Activities and Monitoring Progress

(The parallel section of Chapter 4 gives suggestions for implementing each student's instructional program in each course and for monitoring the student's progress in each course.)

Implementation Activities

Advisors meet in small groups at regularly scheduled times throughout the year to plan and to increase their skill in conducting the individual conferences.

Each advisor plans each of his or her advisee's program, monitors the student's progress in all courses, and evaluates the student's completed program.

a. Developing the student's educational plan.

Assess the student's learning characteristics. Examine the student's educational record—achievement, attendance, and similar information; mental ability scores; norm-referenced achievement test scores; criterion-referenced test scores; self-concept; attitudes toward peers, teachers, classes, learning; aptitude for academic learning; interests; learning styles; family situation; and any unusual gifts or learning problems.

Assess the student's educational needs. From records or in the first planning conference, assess the student's needs in terms of what will be helpful to the student while in school and, if feasible, after high school graduation.

Acquaint all advisees with requirements and options. Meet with advisees as a group to inform them of requirements and options. Follow school procedures for getting the same information to each student's parents.

Conduct first planning conference with each student. Student and advisor outline a tentative plan that includes a schedule of classes, extracurricular activities, and study periods and/or homework schedule.

Conduct conference with student and parents. Modify initial plan, if necessary. Student sets a goal for each course in terms of the letter grade intended. The schedule of homework is finalized. This plan is signed by the student, the parents, and the advisor and each receives a copy.

b. Monitoring the student's progress in all courses and other activities.

Informally monitor each student's progress in each course in small-group discussions and individual sessions with the students as part of the homeroom activities. Formally monitor each student's progress by examining (a) grades assigned in relation to goals set, (b) teachers' reports of any student experiencing difficulty at any time before grades are assigned, and (c) volunteer reports of the student or the student's parents.

Confirm satisfactory progress with oral and written comments and confer individually with the student and with the student's teacher when a difficulty is experienced.

Encourage and aid each student in self-monitoring of progress and reporting any problems to the advisor.

c. Evaluating the student's completed program.

Compare the semester grades and the teachers' comments of one high-achiever, one middle-achiever, and one low-achiever, with the goals set by the student. In a conference with each student and the parents, discuss the appropriateness of each course and other activity in relation to the student's learning characteristics and the value of each course to the student in relation to the student's educational needs.

Monitoring Implementation of the Strategy

A member of the task force monitors the schoolwide implementation of the strategy, using the following information-gathering, feedback, and assistance procedures:

Information gathering--examining students' educational plans, meeting periodically with advisors, conferring with advisors, and conferring with students and their parents.

Confirming exemplary practices and overcoming difficulties--conferring with the advisors of a department or a grade as a group, conferring with individual advisors, providing on-call assistance to an advisor, involving individual advisors and groups of advisors in sharing information regarding their progress and problems, and securing assistance as needed from task force members, central office staff, or other sources.

The task force establishes a recognition program for all advisors who demonstrate excellence in implementing the individual educational programming strategy.

9. Evaluation in Terms of Goal Attainment and Effectiveness of Implementing the Strategy

The purposes of the evaluation are solely to improve students' educational programs and the implementation of the educational programming strategy, not to arrive at judgments that influence teachers' salaries or job security in any way. Accordingly, a task force member who is not responsible for evaluating teachers' performances coordinates the activities.

Determining the extent to which each student had an appropriate educational program each semester.

Each advisor and the student will examine the student's completed educational program and achievement based on letter grades, test results, etc., to judge how appropriate and worthwhile

53

each course was for the student in terms of the student's capability for learning the particular subject matter, interests, career goals, learning styles, and other characteristics.

Each advisor's evaluations will be summarized and used in determining the extent to which all the students had appropriate and worthwhile educational programs. Based on all the evaluations, each advisor will make recommendations regarding changes in the curriculum, instruction, and other aspects of schooling. These recommendations will be reviewed and included in the annual report.

<u>Determining the effects of individual educational programming on student achievement.</u>

Each advisor will use teacher grades and test results to determine the extent to which each advisee attained his or her achievement goals.

Test results, grade point average, and other information will be examined for the composite group of students of each grade to ascertain the extent to which the students attained the achievement goals set for each grade.

<u>Determining how well the strategy was implemented.</u>

In addition to the preceding information, advisors will respond to a questionnaire that has items pertaining to advisors' being provided necessary information regarding curricular and extracurricular offerings and requirements and each student's educational needs and learning characteristics. Advisors will also respond to items addressed to identifying effective practices and problems that were experienced. A questionnaire will be administered to students and to parents to gain their views.

A report will be prepared summarizing the implementation of the individual educational programming strategy and possible improvements to be made in it. The report will be prepared in such a manner that the results cannot be related to individual students or individual teachers.

10. Refinement and Renewal

Based on the evaluation, ineffective practices and schooling arrangements will be eliminated and effective practices and schooling arrangements will be maintained and strengthened. As the staff continues to implement the strategy and as more sophisticated staff development continues, the school will strengthen its own improvement capability and the staff will experience continuing renewal as a social organization.

11. Time Schedule

See Chapter 1 for suggestions for developing a time schedule.

12. Budget

See Chapter 1 for suggestions for preparing a budget.

Improvement Plan—Refining the Individual Educational Programming Strategy, 1984-85: Webster Transitional School, Cedarburg, WI

(Enrollment 652 in grades 6-8 in 1983-84.)

1. Title

Refining the Implementation of the Individual Educational Programming Strategy.

2. Need

In the first week of school, 70% of the grade 8 students passed 80% or more of the subtests of the mathematics K-8 Performance Based Education (PBE) objectives and 72% passed 80% or more of the tests for the PBE reading objectives. On the California Test of Basic Skills (CTBS) administered in grade 7, most of the scores of each student in language arts, science, social studies, and use of references were above expectations, based on mental ability. However, 25% of the students had scores on one or more tests below expectation. In general, the grade 7 teachers' judgments about the entering grade 8 students supported the test results. Accordingly, each grade 8 teacher, working with the other teachers of the grade 8 team, will use the test results and grade 7 teachers' judgments in planning an appropriate total academic program in language skills, reading, mathematics, science, and social studies for each student and in monitoring each student's progress.

3. Percent of Students and Grades Involved

100% of the students in grade 8.

4. Persons Who Will Coordinate and Evaluate the Refinement

A task force consisting of the principal, instructional consultant, reading consultant, and a teacher from each of the three grade 8 academic teams.

5. Persons Who Will Implement the Program

The teachers of each of the grade 8 academic and instruction units. Each teacher also serves as an advisor to part of the students of the unit.

6. Improvement Goals

General Goal

Each grade 8 student will have an educational program that will enable him or her to work on and complete all of the K-8 PBE objectives in math and reading and to achieve at expectancy or higher in each other academic subject.

Performance Goal

90% of more grade 8 students will complete all of the K-8 PBE math and reading objectives by the end of grade 8.

90% or more grade 8 students will be rated by their teachers as having achieved at or above expectancy in each other academic subject.

7. Preparatory Activities

Examine each entering grade 8 student's cumulative record that includes PBE scores for grades 6 and 7 and other information.

Examine the computer printout of the CTBS results to identify each student's achievement in relation to expectancy on each subtest.

Administer the PBE tests in mathematics and reading in the first week of school and prepare each grade 8 student's profile of test scores.

Examine how each grade 8 teacher arranged instruction last year to take into account each grade 8 student's PBE scores (grade 7 CTBS scores were not available).

8. First-Year Implementation Activities and Monitoring Progress

Implementation Activities

Place the students in four mathematics groups based on their PBE math scores and in four reading groups based on their PBE reading scores.

Inform each student and the student's parents of the math objectives and the reading objectives that the student should master during grade 8.

Provide whole-group instruction for objectives that no students have mastered and small-group and individual activities for objectives that some students yet need to master.

Place the students in heterogeneous groups in social studies and in four groups in language and in science according to their achievement scores on the grade 7 CTBS and the grade 7 teacher judgments.

Inform each student and the student's parents of the student's status as being above or below expectancy in grade 7.

Carry out whole-group, small-group, and individual instruction in language, science, and social studies as appropriate for each student to attain his or her course objectives.

Change students' groupings depending upon their achievement at the end of each nine weeks.

All grade 6-8 teachers of each department meet monthly to share ideas regarding materials and techniques pertaining to each PBE objective.

Monitoring Progress

Formally check each student's progress in each subject every four weeks, and share the information with other members of the team.

Share information each four weeks with other team members regarding successful teaching techniques and use of materials.

Inform parents at the end of the third quarter regarding their child's progress. Indicate to the parents whether or not, based on present progress, their child will be recommended for summer school as a means of aiding the child in mastering all the PBE mathematics objectives, reading objectives, or both.

Indicate to parents the mathematics and reading objectives their child has not mastered and indicate how long (one week to six weeks) the child will probably need to master the remaining objectives.

9. Evaluation in Terms of Goal Attainment and Effectiveness of the Strategy

Administer the PBE mathematics and reading tests in June to determine the number of objectives each grade 8 student mastered.

Secure the teachers' estimates of the extent to which each student achieved up to expectancy in language, science, social studies, and study skills.

Review the educational programs of a sample of the high-achieving, middle-achieving, and low-achieving boys and girls. Confer with the students individually to identify the extent to which their programs were appropriate for them in terms of their learning characteristics and their educational needs. Use the information in planning the incoming grade 8 students' programs.

10. Refinement

Task force members meet during the summer to relate the test results and teacher ratings to the implementation of the educational programming strategy and to develop a plan for next year. Continue refinement of the planning, implementation, and monitoring as appropriate.

11. Time Schedule

	Starting Date	Ending Date
Preplanning Activities	March 1985	March 1985
Planning	April 1985	September 1985
Preparatory Activities	August 1985	September 1985
First-Year Implementation	September 1985	June 1986
Evaluation of First-Year Implementation	October 1985	August 1986
Refinement and Renewal	August 1986	-----

12. Budget

	Planning and Preparation	First-Year Implementation/ Evaluation	Refinement/ Renewal
Substitute teachers	$640.00	$320.00	$320.00
Summer employment	$500.00	$500.00	$500.00
Consultants			
Workshops, seminars, etc.			
Materials, tests, etc.			
Travel			
Other			

Chapter 4
Improving Instruction:
Teacher Involvement Is the Key

Rationale

Focus on the Individual Student

Conditions for Effective Instruction

Design Objectives

Preplanning Activities

Prototypic Plan

Improvement Plan—Reading Vocabulary Improvement, 1984-85:
Webster Transitional School, Cedarburg, WI

Improvement Plan—
Using the Computer as a Teaching Tool, 1984-85-86:
Stevens Point Area High School, Stevens Point, WI

Rationale

Many teachers are providing excellent instruction to each student enrolled in their courses. However, knowledge and technology are increasing very rapidly, and the worlds of work and family and social life are changing even more rapidly. Accordingly, we recognize the need for continually improving instruction in order to enable the present generation of students to succeed while in school and to prepare themselves for fruitful living as adults.

Focus on the Individual Student

Instructional programming for the individual student is a major strategy for improving schooling. Its focus is on the individual student rather than the classroom as a group. It is a three-phase strategy (see Chapter 4 of text for a detailed explanation). First, the teacher plans an instructional program with each student enrolled in his or her courses during the first week of the course. The student's instructional plan includes a list of the course objectives the student will try to attain, an indication of the type of activities and materials the student will use to attain the objectives, and an indication of the assessment tools and procedures that will be employed. Other instructional activities are carried out during this same time.

In the second phase of individual instructional programming, the teacher provides learning activities that aid the student in attaining his or her objectives and regularly monitors the student's progress. Monitoring is done to provide feedback to the student, to recognize and encourage the student for learning well, to identify difficulties a student may be experiencing, and to aid the student in overcoming the difficulties.

In the last week of each semester, the teacher implements the third phase of the strategy. This involves the teacher and the student in evaluating the appropriateness and value of the course for the student (see p. 176 of the text for a student opinionnaire regarding course work). The teacher uses this information to arrange better programs for incoming students and to improve the course.

Individual _instructional_ programming cannot be implemented effectively if a student is placed in a course that is inappropriate, that is, if the individual _educational_ programming strategy (see Chapter 3) is not implemented effectively. A student who is found to be placed in an inappropriate course or unit is reassigned.

Individual instructional programming does not imply all one-to-one instruction or only individual projects or assignments. To the contrary, any student's instructional program in any given course may include teacher-directed individual, small-group, and whole-class activities and student-initiated individual, small-group, and whole-class activities.

Conditions for Effective Instruction

Individual instructional programming is a global strategy for improving instruction, not a particular method of teaching. The strategy implies that there is no one method of teaching that is appropriate for all courses, all students, and all teachers. Contrariwise, how the strategy is implemented varies greatly according to the nature of the course being taught, the nature of the students taking the course, the material resources for teaching the particular course, and the philosophy and competencies of the teacher.

Nature of the Course

The extent to which the students have different instructional programs in any given course is dependent on three features of the course:

Whether all or only some of the course objectives are identical for all of the students.

Whether the students must attain the course objectives to a mastery criterion or whether the student may proceed to the next unit or course without attaining mastery.

Whether or not the students must meet a specified achievement level to be enrolled in the course.

The students enrolled in a course will have instructional programs most alike when the course objectives are identical for all students and when the students must reach the same mastery criterion and must have already met a specified achievement level to be enrolled in the course. Courses arranged specifically to enable students to reach specified minimum competency requirements in mathematics, English, reading, and writing are representative of this type of course. Although the instructional programs of all the students are alike in terms of objectives and mastery criteria, the learning activities should not be identical. Rather, different learning paths, instructional materials, and learning activities should be arranged to accommodate differences among the students in

64

interests, learning styles, learning strategies, and other characteristics.

Nature of the Students

A number of factors regarding the students influence the ease and effectiveness of planning an appropriate instructional program for each student, monitoring each student's progress, and evaluating the student's programs:

The extent to which the students want to learn the course content.

The extent to which the students are well behaved.

The extent to which students attend class regularly.

Teachers have a powerful influence on student motivation, conduct, and attendance. However, the differences between students of different high schools in the preceding characteristics are probably as great as the differences among teachers in their influence on students. In a school where student motivation for learning is high, conduct is good, and attendance is regular, individual instructional programming is implemented readily. On the other hand, in schools where student interest in academic learning is low, undisciplined conduct is the typical behavior, and attendance is poor, it is impossible to arrange appropriate instructional programs for every student.

In all schools, teachers need leadership and support from the principal, the district office, and parents in establishing a desirable learning environment. In a school such as the latter one above, the leadership and support are prerequisite to effective instructional programming.

Resources for Teaching

Arranging an excellent instructional program for each student requires material resources for teaching and time arrangements, including:

An adequate amount of space and flexible furniture.

An adequate amount of high quality equipment.

An adequate amount of high quality instructional materials and supplies.

Appropriate facilities and time during school hours for planning as an individual teacher and as a member of a mutual-interest group of teachers.

In general, principals and teachers recognize the importance of equipment, supplies, and materials. However, they often are unaware of the amount of time that is needed for individual planning and preparation and for small-group planning and cooperative problem solving.

Philosophy and Competencies of the Teacher

Employment of the instructional programming strategy as a means of continually improving instruction is facilitated by the teacher's:

Openness to new ideas.

Willingness to work with other teachers.

Recognition of each student's need to experience success on learning tasks.

Ensuring that each student learns well rather than that all students cover identical course content.

Competence in using class time to plan students' instructional programs, to monitor progress, and to aid students in overcoming difficulties.

Competence in using the material resources of the school and the intellectual resources of the students in arranging appropriate instructional programs for the students.

Competence in arranging more than one learning path for students to attain the same objective.

Leadership and support by the principal and the district office are essential for continually improving instruction. One means of identifying the kind of leadership and support needed is for the principal to find out from teachers whether a desired school and classroom learning environment in terms of the student characteristics mentioned earlier is being arranged and whether the resources for teaching are being supplied. In addition to these essential conditions for effective instruction, a continuing program of inservice/staff development activities directed specifically toward meeting the teachers' expressed needs is essential. These ideas are clarified later in this chapter.

Design Objectives

Comprehensive Objective

An individual instructional program that takes into account the student's aptitudes, interests, motivation, learning styles, career goals, and other personal and social characteristics is arranged for the student in each course and in any other activity that is part of the student's total educational program.

Illustrative Enabling Objectives

The instructional program of the student:

Is planned by the student and the teacher of the course at the beginning of the course.

Includes course and unit objectives that are appropriate for the student in terms of the student's aptitude, entering achievement level, and career goals.

Provides an appropriate amount of time in class and during or outside school hours to suit the student's rate of achieving his or her objectives in the course.

Provides for appropriate individual attention by the teacher to take into account the student's motivation and other personality characteristics.

Provides for an appropriate amount of **teacher-directed** individual, pair, small-group, and large-group activity to take into account the student's need for structure and preferences for mode of instruction.

Provides for an appropriate amount of **student-initiated** individual, pair, small-group, and large-group activity to take into account the student's need for independence and preferences for mode of instruction.

Provides for appropriate use of printed materials, audiovisual materials, and direct experiencing to take into account the student's preferred styles of learning—visual, auditory, tactual, or kinesthetic.

Preplanning Activities

Either the members of the Educational Improvement Committee or a task force on arranging an appropriate instructional program for each student carry out preplanning activities such as the following:

View and discuss the filmstrip "Educational Programming for the Individual Student in Secondary Schools: Part II."

Listen to and discuss relevant sections of the audiocassette "Experiences of Two Middle Schools and Two Senior High Schools with Individual Programming for the Individual Student: Part II."

Read textbook Chapter 4, "Instructional Programming for the Individual Student."

Visit schools that are implementing individual instructional programming, confer with other schools by phone and mail, and secure curriculum guides and other printed material on individual instructional programming.

Assess their school's present situation, identify possible improvements in instructional practices, outline possible means of implementing the improvements, determine the inservice education that will be needed and whether it will be conducted by the school staff or secured from an external source, and estimate the costs of planning, preparation, and implementation.

Gain faculty and parent commitment to implementing individual instructional programming.

Prototypic Plan

The members of either the Educational Improvement Committee or a task force on instructional programming for the individual student prepare the plan. Other teachers, parents, students, and other persons are invited to participate in relevant aspects of the planning process. A district official serves as an ad hoc member of the task force or as a consultant to it.

1. Title

   Implementing the Individual Instructional Programming Strategy.

2. Need for Individual Instructional Programming

   A continuing instructional survey shows that the instructional programs of the students in some courses are uniformly excellent. However, the instructional programs of some students are inappropriate in terms of the students' learning characteristics and their educational needs. The progress of many students for whom a course is appropriate is not being monitored in such a way that they are learning as well as they might, nor are they using the entire class period to learn. Moreover, the instructional programs of the students in some courses are not improving from one semester to the next.

3. Percent of Students and Grades Involved

   100% of the students of each grade.

4. Persons Who Will Coordinate and Evaluate the Implementation of the Strategy

   The task force on individual instructional programming.

5. Persons Who Will Implement the Strategy

   All teachers.

6. Improvement Goals

General Goal

   Each student, and accordingly the composite group of students in each course, will have an instructional program that is appropriate for the student in terms of the student's educational needs and learning characteristics--entering achievement level, motivation, general interests, career goals, and learning styles.

Performance Goals

   Each student of each grade will have an appropriate instructional program in each course in which he or she is enrolled.

   100% of the students in each grade will have appropriate instructional programs in each course in which they are enrolled.

General Goal

Each student, and accordingly the composite group of students of each grade, will achieve high in the academic subjects in terms of capability for learning the course material.

Performance Goals

Each student will achieve as high as expected in each subject as measured by a norm-referenced test.

10% more students of each grade this year than last year will meet the minimum requirement (criterion) for high school graduation in English, mathematics, reading, and writing.

Each student who attends class regularly and makes a reasonable effort to learn will be given a grade of C or higher.

7. Preparatory Activities

Arrange the planning group's teaching schedules and provide substitute teachers as necessary so that the planning group can meet at regularly scheduled times during the school day.

Arrange for the planning group to meet outside school hours as necessary to attend workshops, to gain information, and to plan.

Develop guidelines and forms for use by teachers and students in planning each student's instructional program, monitoring the student's progress, and evaluating the student's completed instructional program.

Aid the teachers in preparing to implement the individual instructional programming strategy by studying the WRISE and other materials, visiting schools that have exemplary practices, and arranging for inservice activities.

Prepare guidelines for teachers to use in selecting and developing instructional materials and evaluation tools and techniques.

Arrange for teachers to prepare some of their teaching aids and evaluation procedures prior to starting to teach their courses.

8. First-Year Implementation Activities and Monitoring the
   Implementation of the Strategy

Implementation Activities

Individual teachers and teachers with mutual interests meet at a regularly scheduled time during school hours to plan, develop materials, and increase their skills in all aspects of individual instructional programming.

During the first week of class each student and the teacher plan the student's instructional program. The program specifies course and unit objectives that are appropriate for the student in terms of the student's learning characteristics and educational needs.

Each teacher aids each student in attaining his or her objectives using techniques such as the following:

Planning each lesson carefully.

Providing clear, focused instruction each day.

Arranging learning activities of an appropriate level of difficulty for each student and expecting the student to learn well.

Providing appropriate amounts of time during class or outside school hours to suit each student's rate of achieving his or her objectives.

Arranging for enrichment and acceleration for rapid learners and reteaching and relearning for slow learners.

Providing for appropriate individual attention to take into account differences among students in motivation and other learning characteristics.

Providing for an appropriate amount of teacher-directed individual, pair, small-group, and large-group activity to meet different course objectives and to take into account differences among students in their needs for structure and preferences for mode of instruction.

Providing for an appropriate amount of student-initiated individual, pair, small-group, and large-group activity to meet different course objectives and to take into account differences among students in their needs for independence and preferences for mode of instruction.

Providing for appropriate use of printed materials, audio-visual materials, and direct experiencing to take into account each student's preferred styles of learning--visual, auditory, tactual, or kinesthetic.

Maintaining positive personal interactions with each student.

Recognizing and rewarding each student for excellence in attaining his or her objectives.

Maintaining effective classroom management techniques.

The teacher formally and informally monitors each student's progress toward attaining his or her unit and course objectives using various information gathering, feedback, and correction procedures:

Information gathering--observing the student's classroom performances, rating work samples, administering teacher-constructed tests, administering published norm-referenced and criterion-referenced tests, involving the student in self-testing.

Feedback and correction--informal classroom interaction with the student, individual conferences with the student, conferences with the student and the student's parents, involving the student in self-initiated feedback and correction.

Matching grading procedures with the primary goals of monitoring, i.e., to ensure student success and to avoid student failure.

Toward the end of the semester, the teacher measures each student's attainment of the teacher's course objectives and the student's course goals, using relevant information-gathering techniques.

The teacher evaluates each student's completed instructional program in terms of its appropriateness and value. Appropriateness is based on the student's program having taken into account the student's learning characteristics. Value is based on the program having met the student's educational needs, now as a student and in the future as a citizen, as perceived by the student and the student's parents.

Monitoring Implementation of the Strategy

A member of the task force monitors the schoolwide implementation of the strategy using the following information-gathering, feedback, and assistance procedures:

Information-gathering--examining student's instructional plans; conferring with students and their parents; meeting periodically with the teachers of a department or grade level; examining grade reports, teachers' comments, test results, and attendance records; and observing classrooms.

Confirming exemplary practices and overcoming difficulties-- conferring informally with the teachers of a grade or a department, conferring with individual teachers, making available on-the-spot assistance upon teacher request, involving individual teachers and mutual-interest groups of teachers in sharing information regarding their own progress and problems, and securing assistance from task force members, the district office, or other sources.

The task force establishes a recognition program for all teachers who demonstrate excellence in implementing the individual instructional programming strategy.

9. Evaluation

Comment: The purpose of evaluation (as of the preceding monitoring) is solely to improve instruction, not to arrive at judgments that influence teachers' salaries or job security in any way. Accordingly, a task force member who is not responsible for evaluating teachers' performances coordinates the activities.

Ensuring that teachers have secured the information needed for planning and monitoring and that instructional conditions were arranged so that the teachers could implement the instructional programming strategy effectively.

Each teacher will complete a short checklist rating the extent to which the student information was provided at the beginning of each course and instructional conditions were arranged to facilitate individual instructional programming. A task force member will summarize the results of the ratings for each subject field. This information will be used in assessing the implementation of the instructional programming strategy for the current year and in setting goals and planning improvements for the next year.

Determining the extent to which each student had an appropriate instructional program in the course.

At the time of reporting the semester grade, each teacher will provide a summary indicating the percentage of students of each course who had appropriate instructional programs. (See p. 176 of the text for a student questionnaire regarding course appropriateness.) A task force member will collate the teachers' summaries according to subject field and grade of school. This information will be used along with earlier monitoring data in assessing how well the instructional programming strategy was implemented with the students of each grade in each subject.

Determining the effects of instructional programming in terms of student outcomes.

A task force member will examine relevant standardized and criterion-referenced test results, grades, and other information to ascertain the extent to which the students in each course and in each subject field attained the achievement goals that were set. This information will also be used in setting goals, planning related improvements, and refining the instructional programming strategy.

A report will be prepared summarizing the effectiveness of instruction and of the implementation of the individual instructional programming strategy. Possible improvements will be recommended. The report will be prepared in such a manner that the results cannot be related to individual students or individual teachers.

10. Refinement and Renewal

Based on the evaluation, instruction and related schooling arrangements will be improved and the individual instructional programming strategy will be refined. As the teachers continue to implement the strategy and as more sophisticated staff development continues, the school will strengthen its self-improvement capability and the staff will experience continuing renewal as a social organization.

11. Time Schedule

See Chapter 1 for developing a time schedule.

12. Budget

See Chapter 1 for preparing a budget.

Improvement Plan—Reading Vocabulary Improvement, 1984-85: Webster Transitional School, Cedarburg, WI

Improvement Plan

1. Title

Reading Vocabulary Improvement.

2. Need

A district curriculum committee identified vocabulary development as a problem, elementary school into high school. The Webster Instructional Improvement Committee examined the results of locally constructed performance-based tests and the Gates-MacGinitie Reading Test and found vocabulary scores to be lower than desired.

3. Percent of Students and Grades Involved

100% of all students in grades 6-8.

4. Persons Who Planned and Will Coordinate and Evaluate the Program

Principal, reading consultant, instructional consultant, and members of the Instructional Improvement Committee.

5. Persons Who Will Implement the Activities

All Webster faculty.

6. Improvement Goals

General Goal

The students of grades 6-8 will increase their vocabularies and will integrate new and old vocabulary into their speaking, listening, and writing vocabularies.

Performance Goal

The mean percentile of each quartile in mental ability of each grade in the spring of 1985 will be the same as or higher than it was in the spring of 1984 as measured by the Gates-MacGinitie Reading Test.

7. Preparatory Activities

   Teachers of each subject at inservice sessions:

   Brainstorm ideas.

   Preview available computer software:

   Software for increasing vocabulary.

   Word processing for use in connection with increasing the variety of words.

   Examine available curriculum materials:

   Scrabble, Password, Probe, Boggle, Crypto, and Bali.

   Basic Thinking Skills - Analogies Book C & D.

   Working with Analogies.

   Reading and Thinking Skills.

   Vocabulary Building in Young Adults.

   ITV Wordsmith Videotapes.

   Share teacher-made activities and ideas:

   Teacher developed games--dictionary, flashcards for general words, Vocabulary Tournament (flash cards for science, social studies, current events), IMC Word a Day.

   Content areas--teach vocabulary related to specific units, use thesaurus and Dictionary of Synonyms and Antonyms, use the computer area for word processing, use filmstrip or cassette on using thesaurus.

   Participate in inservice session with consultant, Dr. Carl Personke.

   Meet as a total faculty at end of the inservice activities to discuss activities.

   Academic teams, allied arts team, and EEN teachers during regular meeting times identify which ideas to implement and plan to implement them.

8. First-Year Implementation Activities and Monitoring Progress

Implementation Activities

Carry out the activities as planned.

Spend additional time as necessary on instruction designed to attain performance goals.

Insure that each student uses materials and gets instruction in line with his or her interests.

Try to keep each student on task throughout the time allocated for instruction.

Encourage students to read and talk outside of the regularly scheduled class time.

Monitoring Progress

Each academic teacher will monitor the progress of assigned students on a regular basis.

Each teacher will include a discussion of the student's progress in the regularly scheduled student-parent-advisor conferences.

Each academic team, the allied arts team, and EEN teachers will discuss progress and problems in their regularly scheduled meetings.

The principal and instructional coordinator will meet periodically with each team to receive reports of progress and to aid the team in its implementation activities and in monitoring progress.

The District Director of Instruction will discuss progress as time permits in his scheduled school visits and will aid the school in its implementation activities and monitoring progress.

9. Evaluation in Terms of Goal Attainment and Effectiveness of Activities

At the end of each grading period, teachers will systematically estimate the extent to which each student is making progress toward increasing the size of his or her vocabulary and toward integrating the new vocabulary into his or her speaking, listening, and writing vocabulary.

At the last grading period of the year, each academic team will estimate the extent to which their students attained the above goal.

The mean percentile score of each quartile of each grade and each individual student's test score on the Gates-MacGinitie Reading Test will be examined in the spring of 1985 to ascertain whether it was as high as or higher than in the spring of 1984.

10. Refinement

Modifications based on the 1984-85 evaluation will be incorporated into the 1985-86 activities.

11. Time Schedule

	Starting Date	Ending Date
Preplanning	August 27, 1984	September 4, 1984
Planning	September 5, 1984	September 28, 1984
Preparatory Activities	October 1984	March 1985
Baseline-Year Evaluation	1983-84	1983-84
First-Year Implementation	October 1984	June 1985
Evaluation of First-Year Implementation	October 1984	Fall 1985
Refinement and Renewal	1985-86	

12. Budget

Money has been allocated for inservice. Money for computers and software is provided for in the Block Grant and in the computer software budget.

Improvement Plan—
Using the Computer as a Teaching Tool, 1984-85-86: Stevens Point Area High School, Stevens Point, WI

1. Area of Improvement

Using the Computer in High School as a Teaching Tool.

2. Need for Improvement

Computer literacy is taught in grades K-6. Computer programming is taught in grades 7-12, and CAI is used in some curriculum areas in grades 7-12. This project is directed toward each grade

10-12 teacher using the computer to provide more effective instruction for individual students enrolled in his or her courses, not to provide whole-class instruction.

A survey of the high school teachers indicated a desire to use microcomputers in this way. Approximately 25% of the teachers of grades 10-12 will make some use of computers in 1984-85 and 100% will in 1985-86.

3. Percent of Students and Grades Involved

25% of the students in 1984-85, all who are enrolled in classes of teachers who use the computer.

4. Persons Who Planned and Will Coordinate and Evaluate the Project

A high school task force on computer utilization consisting of an art teacher, an English teacher, a reading specialist teacher, the director of the IMC, the vocational education coordinator, and the chairpersons of the mathematics, business education, computer education, science, and social studies departments. Ad hoc members include the high school principal, the district curriculum administrator, and the district administrator of media and technology.

5. Persons Who Will Implement the Activities

In 1984-85, 25% of the teachers under the leadership of their respective department chairpersons.

6. Improvement Goals

General Goal

All students who are enrolled in classes of the teachers using the computer will attain course content more readily and will show higher interest in their course work.

Performance Goals

Each student enrolled in a course in which the computer is used will either acquire more course content in the same time or acquire the same content in less time, as reported in a teacher questionnaire and a student questionnaire.

Each student enrolled in a course in which the computer is used will indicate higher interest in the course as reported in a teacher questionnaire and a student questionnaire.

Each volunteer teacher will increase his or her competence in use of the computer as a teaching tool as reported in a teacher questionnaire and reflected in the teacher's computer lesson summaries.

7. Preparatory Activities

Organize a task force on computer utilization; the task force members attend a 2 1/2 day workshop (Wisconsin Program for the Renewal and Improvement of Secondary Education) and meet bi-weekly to plan and consider other committee tasks, including those that follow:

Survey all instructional staff on the status of computer needs and the status of their personal competency and/or interest in using computers.

Conduct district computer literacy inservice seminars for high school teachers. Seminars involve 12 hours of instruction for each participating teacher.

Involve all staff in selection of computer hardware and software.

Recommend the purchase of the desired hardware and software.

8. First-Year Implementation Activities and Monitoring Progress

Implementation Activities

Volunteer teachers utilize the computer as a teaching tool in lessons of each course. Each lesson is summarized and submitted to the department chairperson. Lesson example:

Subject: Physics

Lesson: Measure the Mechanical Equivalent of Heat

Lesson Summary: It is possible to measure the mechanical equivalent of heat (i.e., the number of joules of mechanical energy in a calorie of heat energy) by measuring the heat gained by lead shot which has been dropped from a known height. In prior semesters, this was done by measuring the initial and final temperature of the lead with a thermometer. The greatest error of the experiment was the heat radiated to the environment from the lead. By using a temperature probe interfaced with an Apple computer, the temperature is measured more accurately. In addition the computer takes the measurements and constructs a graph of the temperature vs. time which clearly illustrates the radiation of the lead shot.

Monitoring Progress

Department chairpersons review the lesson summaries that the teachers of the respective departments provide. Department chairpersons and other members of the task force confer periodically with the teachers to confirm desired practices and to aid teachers who wish assistance.

The principal observes teachers' classrooms and confers with the teacher after the observation.

9. Evaluation in Terms of Goal Attainment and Effectiveness of Activities

Administer a questionnaire to the computer-usage teachers in May that addresses the performance goals regarding student achievement, student interest, and teacher competence in computer usage.

Administer a questionnaire to the students that addresses student achievement and student interest.

Interview a random sample of teachers and a random sample of students of these teachers' classes to gain more detailed information about effective computer use.

Analyze all the lesson summaries to identify possible trends in more frequent and/or more effective use of computers.

Collate all the data and summarize the results.

10. Refinement

The evaluation results will be shared with all teachers and submitted to the Stevens Point District Improvement Committee. The results will be used in developing the computer usage plan for 1986-87.

11. Time Schedule

	Starting Date	Ending Date
Preparatory Activities	October 1983	December 1984
First-Year Partial Implementation	October 1984	June 1985
First-Year Evaluation	August 1984	June 1985
First-Year Full Implementation	August 1985	June 1986
Refinement	June 1986	Ongoing

12. Budget

$17,000.00 for computer hardware from October 1, 1984, to December 15, 1984.

$1,254.00 for initial software from January 1, 1985, to April 1, 1985.

$6,084.00 for software from May 1, 1985, to December 15, 1985.

Chapter 5
Updating the Curriculum: An Annual Priority

Rationale

Curriculum improvement calls for a cooperative effort by district office and local school staff. Curriculum improvement by a local school staff is necessarily carried out in the context of the district and state requirements and guidelines.

Curriculum Development Strategy

Changing the school's curriculum is accomplished in different ways. One approach employed by local school staff has six major phases:

1. Examine the school's statement of program goals in relation to the district's goals and philosophy. Reconcile any differences between the two.

2. Examine the objectives of each course in relation to the school's program goals and philosophy. Reconcile any differences between the two.

3. Examine the content of each course in relation to the content of other courses of the same program (subject field) and also of other programs. Identify omissions, unintentional overlapping, and lack of continuity between the courses of the same program area. Identify unintentional overlapping among the courses of the various program areas. Based on the findings provide for better continuity and more integration as appropriate. Drop or add courses as appropriate. Allocate more or less time for instruction for the total program and for one or more courses of the program. Develop or revise curriculum guides as needed.

4. Examine the content of each course in terms of its effectiveness in facilitating the attainment of the course objectives. Identify omissions, overlapping, lack of continuity, and irrelevant content. Provide for better continuity and more integration among units of study within each course as appropriate. Drop or add units of study. Allocate more or less time for units. Develop new unit outlines or update current ones.

5. Examine the content of each course in terms of its providing an appropriate instructional program for each student who typically enrolls in the course. Modify the content as necessary so that it is neither too easy nor too difficult for any student and so that the content meets each student's educational needs.

6. Examine the instructional arrangements, including the methods and materials, in terms of facilitating the attainment of the course objectives and arranging an appropriate instructional program for each student. Consider the quantity, appropriateness, and variety of the materials and the effectiveness of the methods. Make revisions and changes as necessary.

Middle School and High School Curriculum Patterns

Curricula vary considerably from one school district to another and from one state to another. To establish a common frame of reference for considering curriculum improvement, a middle school curriculum, grades 6 through 8, and a high school curriculum, grades 9 through 12, are outlined. The remainder of the chapter is based on these curriculum patterns.

About two-thirds of the middle school day in each of grades 6, 7, and 8 is given to language arts, reading, mathematics, science, and social studies. The remainder of the time across the three grades is given to art, career education, foreign languages, music, physical education and health, and applied arts. However, instruction in no more than three of the last subject fields is provided in any grade during any given week of the year and more instruction is provided in certain areas than in others, e.g., more physical education than career education.

Concerning the high school curriculum, grades 9 through 12, 21 credits are required for graduation and students may take more than 21 credits. Each student to be graduated with a diploma must complete the following requirements, grades 9 through 12:

4 credits in English communication skills and literature

3 credits in social studies

2 credits in mathematics

2 credits in science

1 1/2 credits in the visual and performing arts

1 1/2 credits in health and physical education

1 1/2 credits in career/vocational education and applied arts areas

1/2 credit in computer literacy

5 or more elective credits; foreign language may be part of the electives.

The preceding permits the college preparatory student taking 21 credits to complete 4 credits in English, 3 in social studies, 3 in mathematics, 3 in science, and 3 in a foreign language, a total of 16 credits;, it also requires the student to complete 5 credits in the other four areas. The student taking 21 credits who will seek employment upon high school graduation may complete 4 to 7 credits in a vocational area, 11 to 13 1/2 in English, foreign languages, mathematics, science, and social studies, and 3 1/2 to 6 in the other three areas.

Design Objectives

Comprehensive Objective

Each school's curriculum is based on the district's educational philosophy and the school's program goals. Course goals, course content, and instruction, including materials and methods, are in accord with the district philosophy and the program goals. The school's curriculum is structured to meet state and district requirements but it can be adapted by the school and individual teachers to take into account the differing educational needs of students.

Illustrative Enabling Objectives

The curriculum focuses on student acquisition of knowledge and understanding, skill and competence, attitudes and values, and action patterns in the following programmatic areas:

Communication skills, including reading, writing, speaking, and listening.

Mathematical concepts and skills.

Scientific and technological concepts and skills, including computer technology.

Social science concepts and skills.

The fine and applied arts.

Foreign languages.

Career education, including awareness, exploration, and preparation.

Health education, both physical and mental.

Family and home membership.

Leisure education, including crafts, clubs, and extra-curricular activities.

Related to the preceding areas, curriculum committees, teams of teachers, and individual staff members:

Identify or prepare content outlines.

Identify or formulate course and unit objectives.

Identify or prepare instructional materials, including printed and audiovisual materials, that individual students use to attain their objectives.

Formulate instructional methods, including the use of time and materials, that enable individual students to attain their learning goals.

Ensure that the curriculum offerings and requirements are neither too demanding nor too easy for any student.

Ensure that the course content, the teacher's methods, and the teacher's assessment of student achievement are closely related.

Establish procedures for reporting to the students and parents (and for ensuring a just and fair system of grading if letter grades are reported).

Review and update curriculum content and requirements annually.

Preplanning Activities

Members of the Educational Improvement Committee or of a curriculum improvement task force carry out the following pre-planning activities:

View and discuss the filmstrip "Curricular Patterns in Secondary Schools."

Listen to and discuss relevant sections of the audiocassette "Experiences of a Middle School, a Junior High School, and Two Senior High Schools with Curricular Patterns."

Read textbook Chapter 4, "Curricular Arrangements."

Visit schools that have changed their curriculum; confer with them by phone and mail; and secure curriculum guides, learning guides for students, test manuals, and other printed material.

Assess their school's present curriculum; identify areas for improvement; outline possible means of implementing the improvements; determine the inservice education that will be needed and whether it will be provided by the local school staff or an external source; and estimate the costs of planning, preparation, and implementation.

Prototypic Plan

The members of either the Educational Improvement Committee or a task force on curriculum improvement prepare the school's curriculum improvement plan. Other teachers, parents, students, and other persons are invited to participate in relevant aspects of the planning process. A district official serves as an ad hoc member of the task force or as a consultant to it. The school's plan is based on the district's elementary-high school plan for curriculum improvement.

1. Area of Improvement

Curriculum Improvement in English.

2. Need for Improvement

A needs assessment indicated that many students are taking appropriate work in English and are achieving as high as expected. However, the available English offerings are not appropriate for some students in terms of their entering achievement levels. Too much time is being allocated for certain areas of English and too little for others. Too many students are experiencing failure in English.

3. Percent of Students and Grades Involved

100% of the students of each grade.

4. Persons Who Will Plan, Coordinate, and Evaluate the Activities

The school's Educational Improvement Committee or its task force on English curriculum improvement.

5. Persons Who Will Implement the Activities

All teachers of English and other teachers who require reading, speaking, listening, or writing activities of their students.

6. Improvement Goals

General Goal

The English curriculum offerings will be appropriate for each student, and accordingly for the composite group of students of each grade and the entire school.

Performance Goals

Each student will have appropriate English content and an appropriate amount of time allocated for English instruction.

The English course content and allocated time will be appropriate for 90% or more of the students of each grade.

General Goal

High student achievement in English as determined by norm-referenced or criterion-referenced testing or by teacher grades will be maintained and low achievement will be raised.

Performance Goals

The mean English achievement of students of each grade will equal or exceed the 60th percentile.

90% or more of the students of each grade will meet the desired competency level in English.

Students who attend class regularly and try hard will receive grades of A, B, or C in English.

7. Preparatory Activities

To enable the planning group to develop the improvement plan, arrange the planning group's teaching schedules and provide substitute teachers as necessary so that the planning group can meet at regularly scheduled times during school hours. As necessary, arrange for the planning group to meet outside of school hours to gain information and to plan. In developing the plan, the planning group carries out the six steps given earlier in this chapter and implements relevant design objectives given earlier. The improvement plan will include preparing an English curriculum guide that indicates (a) modifications in the content and/or objectives of existing units and courses, (b) any new units or courses, and (c) an indication of any unit or course to be dropped.

8. First-Year Implementation Activities and Monitoring Progress

Implementation Activities

English teachers and other teachers affected by the curriculum changes meet at regularly scheduled times during school hours, and outside of school hours as necessary, to incorporate the recommendations and materials into their courses.

Inservice/staff development is provided as necessary so that teachers understand and implement the revised curriculum.

Teachers relate the new course content and objectives, their teaching methods and use of materials, and their evaluation devices and procedures.

Teachers aid the students enrolled in their courses in understanding the curriculum goals and objectives.

Teachers adjust the revised curriculum to meet the entering achievement level of each student enrolled in their courses.

Teachers incorporate the curriculum revisions in the instructional programs (see Chapter 4) of the students enrolled in their courses.

Advisors incorporate the curricular revisions in the advisees' educational programs (see Chapter 3) by selecting more appropriate units and/or courses for the students.

Monitoring Progress

Each English teacher monitors the progress of each of the students enrolled in his or her class and at each grading period identifies any student not progressing as well as desired. Students experiencing difficulty are aided in overcoming their problems. Students making excellent progress receive recognition from the teacher.

A member of the task force examines the grades assigned in English. Students making grades lower than desired are identified. The task force member meets with the English teachers whose students are not progressing satisfactorily and works out plans with them for correcting the problem.

A task force member observes English and other teachers' classes and examines the instructional materials and tests they use. If a teacher is experiencing difficulty and desires help, the task force member provides it directly or has other school or district persons provide it.

A task force member secures information from teachers, advisors, and counselors toward the end of the first semester to identify the extent to which the curricular revisions enabled them to arrange more appropriate educational and instructional programs for more students.

9. Evaluation in Terms of Goal Attainment and Effectiveness of Activities

The purpose of the evaluation (as of the preceding monitoring) is solely to determine the effects of the curriculum changes, not to arrive at any judgments that influence teachers' salaries or job security in any way. Accordingly, a task force member who is not responsible for evaluating teachers' performances coordinates the activities.

Ascertaining the extent to which more students had appropriate English course work in their educational programs.

Administer a student checklist and an advisor checklist for this year and last year to identify the appropriateness of the English curriculum for each student. Compare the results. Interview a random sample of the students.

Determining the extent to which already high English achievement was maintained or low achievement was raised.

Compare norm-referenced and criterion-referenced test results and grade-point averages for this year and last year.

Assessing the usability and effectiveness of the curriculum guides and other materials that were developed.

Administer a teacher checklist; interview teachers.

A report will be prepared summarizing the results of the curriculum changes. The report will be prepared in such a manner that results cannot be related to individual students or to individual teachers.

10. Refinement/Renewal

The cycle of assessing the current situation, selecting curriculum elements for improvement, planning, goal setting, implementing, and evaluating improvements to attain the goals will continue on an annual basis. As the staff continues to engage in this cycle of activities and as more sophisticated staff development continues, the school will experience renewal as a social organization.

11. Time Schedule

See Chapter 1 for instructions for developing a time schedule.

12. Budget

See Chapter 1 for instructions for preparing a budget.

Improvement Plan—Curriculum Improvement in English, 1984-85: Steuben Middle School, Milwaukee, WI

Steuben Middle School enrolls about 900 students in grades 7 and 8.

1. Area of Improvement

Curriculum Improvement in Writing Skills.

2. Need for Improvement

A large percentage of the students who take the district mandated writing competency test in grade 9 fail to exhibit adequate writing skills in the testing situation and therefore must be assigned to a remedial class at the high school level. There is a need to identify these students prior to the 9th grade and provide a curriculum which emphasizes the improvement of writing skills.

3. Percent of Students and Grades Involved

Approximately 15% of the grade 7 students and 25% of the grade 8 students in 1984-85.

4. Persons Who Will Plan, Coordinate, and Evaluate the Activities

The central office's Chapter I coordinators with input from the school's principal and learning coordinator will do the initial planning and proposal development. When tentative approval of the proposal is received, English teachers will assist in developing the implementation plan, monitoring student progress, and evaluating the project.

5. Persons Who Will Implement the Activities

One English teacher will teach the students. Support to the teacher will be provided by a central office supervisor, the learning coordinator, and the other English teachers.

6. Improvement Goals

General Goal

Low-achieving grade 7 and grade 8 students will be provided an English curriculum and related instruction designed to enable them to meet the minimum criterion in writing for high school graduation.

Performance Goals

80% of the students will be able to explain the writing, editing, and rewriting process.

80% of the students involved will be able to write an acceptable five-paragraph theme.

90% of the students will exhibit a more positive attitude toward the writing process.

7. Preparatory Activities

Identify the writing teacher and provide training in the desired writing procedures and use of computers for word processing.

The writing teacher and the English teachers identify the students who will be involved in the program.

Identify appropriate space and materials for housing the computers and conducting the class.

Revise the selected students' schedules so that they can take the class.

8. First-year Implementation Activities and Monitoring Progress

Ongoing operation of the program will be the responsibility of the assigned teacher. Support for and monitoring of the program will be provided by the Chapter I supervisor, principal, learning coordinator, and English teachers. The teachers and support personnel will devote sufficient time and energy to insure success of the program.

9. Evaluation in Terms of Goal Attainment and Effectiveness of the Activities

Five types of information will be gathered relating to the writing program:

A writing pretest, administered in September.

Periodic student writing samples.

A writing posttest, administered in late May.

End-of-year student opinions.

End-of-year teacher opinions.

Student's writing samples will be evaluated on the criteria established system-wide for a five-paragraph theme. The holistic scoring methods which are used for the writing competency test will be applied to the student writing samples.

The data gathered will be used to evaluate the goals established for the program for the first year.

Data to be reported to the staff will include the degree of improvement demonstrated by individual students, the average improvement of all students, and the judgments and opinions of the students and English teachers in relation to student attitudes toward writing and the development of writing skills.

10. Refinement

At the end of each year, the writing teacher, Chapter I supervisor, principal, learning coordinator, and English teachers will review the results of the writing samples and opinions gathered. From this review new and/or revised goals and procedures will be developed for the following year.

11. Time Schedule

Initial planning--Semester 2, 1983-84, to develop the proposal for funding.

Planning--Semester 1, 1984-85, to identify and order specific equipment and materials; to develop a system of operation; and to both develop criteria for student involvement in the program and identify the specific students who will be involved.

Implementation--Semester 2, 1984-85. Students will be assigned to classes and instruction will start.

Evaluation—Semester 2, 1984-85. Opinions of the English teachers will be secured related to student improvement. Refinements for the 1985-86 school year will be based on these opinions. Pre- and posttests will be developed and administered during the 1985-86 school year. Future refinements will be based on the results of these tests and teacher opinions.

12. Budget

Initial funding will be provided through the federal government Chapter I program. Local school system funds will not be utilized except for the time involved for the support personnel's involvement in the program. Start-up costs will be high because of the large amount of equipment which must be purchased initially. On-going costs will be less and will continue to be provided from federal funding. Should the federal funds be reduced or eliminated, the local system will assume the expense of operating the program.

Year 1

Equipment:	
15 Apple computers	$12,750
15 cards	1,500
3 printers	1,000
1 25" monitor	800
Software, consumables, etc.	3,000
Total equipment	$19,050
Salary and fringe benefits for one full-time teacher	$32,500
Total estimated cost Year 1	$51,550

Year 2

Salary and fringe benefits for one full-time teacher	$34,000
Software, consumables, etc.	$ 2,000
Total estimated cost Year 2	$36,000

Completed Project—Curriculum Enrichment, 1984-85: Phoenix Middle School, Delavan, WI

Phoenix Middle School enrolls 503 students in grades 5-8.

Persons Who Planned and Monitored the Project

Education Improvement Committee (EIC) consisting of the principal, one guidance counselor, three academic teachers, two allied arts teachers, and one exceptional education teacher.

Goal

Provide more time for instruction in the academic subjects in grades 6-8 and continue a student activity program.

Primary Planning/Implementation Activities

The Saturday Enrichment Program at Phoenix School was implemented through the action of the Phoenix School EIC and the Phoenix School teachers. The Phoenix School has had activity clubs for the past several years that met during the school day. However, the pressure for more time on task led the Phoenix teachers and administration to feel that there must be a better time to provide enrichment activities to our students than during basic skill instruction time. Once the need was established by the Phoenix School EIC, questionnaires were sent to other districts finding out how they carried out activities. Teachers going to conventions and seminars were asked to discuss the concern with fellow attendees to see if we could find a better way of serving our students. The principal found a possible solution at the Middle School Convention in Columbus, Ohio, in November 1984. Two schools represented at that conference described their Saturday Enrichment Program. The Saturday Enrichment Program concept was brought back to the Phoenix School EIC and was received with enthusiasm. The EIC presented the concept to the faculty for their approval. After much discussion, the Saturday Enrichment Program was implemented for the months of March and April 1985. Eleven programs were offered on Saturday mornings, not only for the middle school students of grades 6-8 but also for interested students of grades 9 and 10. The programs were well attended.

Refinement

In the 1985-86 school year these and other enrichment programs will be held on Saturdays during the winter months. There will be a fee of $3.00 to $6.00 to cover administrative costs.

Sample Materials

The following paragraphs are from the program announcement for Winter 1985.

The Phoenix Middle School, Delavan, Wisconsin, is sponsoring a series of courses in a community Saturday Enrichment Program for students in grades 6-10. The classes vary from three to six weeks in length, depending upon the instructors' wishes. In general, the Saturday Enrichment Program begins on March 16 and ends on April 27, 1985.

Registration for the Saturday Enrichment Program will take place from 9:00-11:00 A.M. on Saturday, March 2, 1985. The registration will take place in the Phoenix Middle School lobby. Students must appear in person to register. During the registration process students will be asked to put their name, address, and other important information on the registration sheet for the particular class they desire to participate in. It is advisable that students have more than one class in mind, as there will be a maximum number of students allowed in each class. Classes will be filled on a first come, first served basis.

Please note that there is a small fee for registration in the Saturday Enrichment Program. The program is a community program, so expenses must be met through registration fees. Please be prepared to pay your registration fee in cash. Fee refunds will only be given for cancelled classes. If you have any questions regarding the Saturday Enrichment Program, please call Phoenix School (728-6366) so that your questions may be answered as soon as possible.

Donald J. Carpenter, Program Coordinator
DELAVAN-DARIEN SATURDAY ENRICHMENT PROGRAM

A description of one of 11 courses offered in Winter 1985 follows:

BASIC PHOTOGRAPHY

Saturdays (3) - April 13, 20, 27 (9:00 - 11:00 A.M.)
Open to students in grades 6-10
Instructor - David Austin
Fee $3.00   Room: Phoenix 212

This course will teach the basic principles of photography. Students will learn what makes photography work--the technique and composition of photography and how photography can give you something valuable for your lifetime. Photography can be a useful skill and fun at the same time.

The instructor, David Austin, has operated a photography studio for many years in Delavan. Photography has been his life-long interest.

Chapter 6
Student Decision-Making Arrangements, Self-Discipline, and Citizenship: Democracy Includes Students, Too

Rationale

Design Objectives

Preplanning Activities

Prototypic Plan

Activities Planned To Improve School Climate, 1983-84:
John Burroughs Middle School, Milwaukee WI

Completed Project—Increasing Attendance
by Use of Computer 1984-85:
Wm. Horlick High School, Racine, WI

Rationale

Making wise decisions and accepting the responsibility for one's own actions are essential for self-realization as an individual and for making progress as a group. Wise decision making is learned. Students who do not learn decision-making skills while in school will probably never learn the skills. Similarly, students who are given no opportunity in school for making important decisions and for exercising self-discipline and demonstrating other aspects of good citizenship are unlikely to be ready for meeting these demands successfully upon completing high school.

Some teachers as well as entire faculties hesitate to encourage any student decision making because the school environment is not safe and discipline problems are experienced in most classes. In these situations, corrective actions precede extending student decision making to all students. However, extending student decision making and responsibility to some of the students may be a key element of the corrective program.

Most schools are safe, and discipline, attendance, and other aspects of good citizenship are not problems for teachers or students. In this kind of school, the large majority of students are capable of exercising considerable independence in making decisions regarding their education and conduct without continual supervision and external control.

Improving student decision-making skills and encouraging good citizenship are proposed as a means of fostering a favorable environment for learning and teaching. The administration, faculty, students, and parents formulate the rules governing discipline, grooming, and other student behaviors democratically; and they are all involved in enforcing the rules fairly and justly. Similarly, developing self-disciplined conduct through reasoning, counseling, and modeling is emphasized rather than establishing control over students through a system of rewards and punishments. These propositions are based on the fact that self-disciplined conduct, as well as misconduct, results from the combined effects of the student's home and neighborhood situation, the student's interactions with the school staff and other students, and the student's own values regarding self and schooling.

Design Objectives

Comprehensive Objective:

Students progressively assume more responsibility for learning well, self-disciplined conduct, and good citizenship.

Illustrative Enabling Objectives:

Students in their classes and in meetings with their advisors are taught:

> Decision-making skills that help them to make educational decisions as individuals.
>
> Concepts and skills that enable them to participate in shared decision making with other students, the school staff, and parents.

The individual student exercises increasing initiative for making decisions and accepting the related consequences of the decisions regarding:

> The student's instructional program in each course and his or her total educational program.
>
> The student's conduct, attendance, and other aspects of good citizenship.

Students as members of groups take increasing initiative for making decisions and accepting the responsibility for the decisions regarding:

> The objectives and activities in the course in which the group is enrolled and the extracurricular activity in which the group participates.
>
> The governance of the group.
>
> The school's guidelines regarding attendance, conduct, and other aspects of good citizenship.

Responsible students are encouraged to serve:

> As officers and members of student-governing groups.
>
> As student representatives on the school's standing and ad hoc committees, councils, and task forces.

Preplanning Activities

Members of either the Educational Improvement Committee or a task force on student decision making and citizenship carry out the following preplanning activities:

View and discuss the filmstrip "Student Decision Making in Secondary Schools."

Listen to and discuss relevant sections of the audiocassette "Experiences of a Middle School, a Junior High School, and Two Senior High Schools with Student Decision Making."

Read textbook Chapter 6, "Student Decision-Making Arrangements."

Study the materials of three other components that have direct implications for student decision making: Individual Educational Programming, Individual Instructional Programming, and Career Education and Experiential Learning.

Visit schools that have effective programs, confer with other schools by phone and mail, and secure student conduct guidelines and other materials.

Assess their school's present situation; identify areas of improvement; outline means of implementing the improvements; determine the kind of inservice education that will be needed and whether it will be conducted by the local staff or secured from an external source; and estimate the cost of preparing for, implementing, and continuing the improvements.

Prototypic Plan

The members of either the Educational Improvement Committee or a task force on responsible student decision making and citizenship prepare the improvement plan. Other teachers, parents, students, and other persons are invited to participate in relevant aspects of the planning process. A district official serves as an ad hoc member of the task force or as a consultant to it. The school's plan is based on the district guidelines on student citizenship and conduct.

1. Area of Improvement

   Student Decision-Making Arrangements.

2. Need for Improvement

   A carefully conducted assessment showed that many students are developing individual and group decision-making skills in a desirable manner. They are exercising good citizenship in terms of attendance, punctuality, self-disciplined conduct, interest in academic learning, and positive peer relationships. However, other students are not developing as desired; hence, the climate for learning and teaching is not as positive as desired.

3. Percent of Students and Grades Involved

   100% of the students of each grade.

4. Persons Who Will Coordinate and Evaluate the Activities

   The Educational Improvement Committee or the task force on student decision making.

5. Persons Who Will Implement the Activities

   Administrators, all counselors, all teachers, and selected students.

6. Improvement Goals

General Goal

   Students with each successive year of schooling will improve their skills in making decisions regarding their education.

Performance Goals

   75% of the grade 7 students and 90% of the grade 11 students will be able to apply, when appropriate, a convergent problem-solving model or a divergent (creative) problem-solving model of decision making to problems they experience at school.

   80% of the grade 7 students and 90% of the grade 11 students will take responsibility for planning, monitoring, and evaluating their own instructional programs and their own educational programs with a minimum amount of teacher and advisor guidance.

75% of the grade 7 students and 90% of the grade 11 students will be able to identify instructional materials and activities that are appropriate for them in terms of their ability to read, their interests, and their learning styles, using the list of unit materials and activities presented and discussed by the teacher.

60% of the grade 7 students and 80% of the grade 11 students will be able to select appropriate required and elective units or courses and extracurricular activities when aided by an advisor in an individual conference.

General Goal

Students as members of small groups with each successive year of schooling will take more initiative and assume greater responsibility for conducting the group's learning activities and governing their extracurricular and student activity programs.

Performance Goals

80% of the grade 7 students and 90% of the grade 11 students will learn effectively in small groups of four to six when guided and monitored by a teacher.

60% of the grade 7 students and 95% of the grade 11 students will participate effectively in extracurricular and student activity programs.

General Goal

More students of each successive grade will serve on student and faculty-student committees with increasing effectiveness.

Performance Goals

More student-only committees will function effectively.

More students will serve on faculty-student committees, including improvement committees and task forces.

General Goal

Student citizenship will become more responsible and the resulting school climate will become more positive.

Performance Goals

Tardiness will decrease by 5% and attendance will increase by 2%.

The number of students referred by teachers for discipline reasons will decrease by 10% and the number given in-house and other suspensions will decrease by 20%.

The percentage of dropouts will decrease by 1%.

The number of positive peer relationships outside the classroom will increase by 50%.

The number of students recognized for self-disciplined conduct will increase by 5%.

7. Preparatory Activities

Arrange the planning group's teaching schedule and provide substitute teachers as necessary so that the planning group can meet during regular school hours to develop the improvement plan. As necessary, arrange for the planning group to meet outside school hours to gain information and to plan.

Prepare guidelines pertaining to student decision making, citizenship, and school climate.

Aid the school staff in preparing to use the guidelines and to implement the improvement activities by studying the WRISE materials used earlier as a preplanning activity, arranging for the staff to visit schools that have exemplary practices, making available instructional materials, and arranging for consultants to conduct inservice activities.

8. First-year Implementation Activities and Monitoring Progress

Implementation Activities

Responsible student decision making is increased.

The school offers one or more units of study on decision-making skills.

Counselors and teacher advisors use part of their individual conference sessions with students to encourage the students to make decisions and to teach the students decision-making skills. (See Chapter 5 of the textbook where methods and materials are presented for teaching decision-making skills as part of a program of career education.)

Teachers arrange for pairs and small groups of students to select and manage some group learning activities.

Advisors of extracurricular activities, the student council, and other student activities arrange for students to assume increasing initiative and responsibility for the conduct of these activities and for student self-governance.

Student representatives are placed on student-only and faculty-student committees and task forces.

Attendance is increased by more effective instructional programming for students with a history of absenteeism, counseling absentees, conferring with parents, monitoring attendance at each class by computer and immediate follow-up of absentees with telephone calls to the home, and recognizing good attendance. Punctuality is increased by similar techniques.

Self-disciplined conduct is increased by more effective instructional programming for the individual student; counseling misbehaving students; contacting parents, teachers, counselors, and the administrative team; making clear to students rules of conduct and enforcing the rules; supervision of out-of-class activities and spaces; clearly defined referral procedures; establishment of an in-house detention program for misbehaving students; and recognition of well-behaving students.

The dropout rate is decreased by more effective educational programming and instructional programming that gives attention to a greater range of individual educational needs and learning characteristics; arranging course work and assignments designed specifically to promote academic success; counseling, conferring with parents, peer counseling, and small-group interaction; and programs recognizing the values of completing high school.

Students are recognized for punctuality, regular attendance, self-disciplined conduct, prosocial interactions with peers, and good care of materials and school property by means of PA announcements, letters to parents, display of the student's picture, going on field trips, attending recognition luncheons, personal notes of commendation, on-the-spot reinforcement, and group awards.

Monitoring Progress

Teachers monitor student citizenship daily and prepare a summary report at the end of each grading period. Desired student actions are recognized. The teachers, with assistance of a task force member, work out corrective programs for students with undesirable records. Students with acute or chronic problems are referred to a counselor or other school or district official.

A task force member observes classes, individual conferences, and extracurricular and other student activities; confers with staff, students, and parents; and examines records. Effective teacher and advisor practices are reinforced and plans are worked out to correct the ineffective.

A task force member observes classes and individual conferences, examines records, and observes group meetings of students
and teachers or advisors. If a staff member is experiencing
difficulty and desires assistance, the task force member provides
it directly or has other school or district persons provide it.

Teachers discuss their progress and concerns with a task force
member.

9. Evaluation in Terms of Goal Attainment and Effectiveness of
   Improvement Activities

The purpose of the evaluation activities that follow, and also
of the preceding monitoring, is solely to improve student decision
making and citizenship, not to arrive at judgments that influence
teachers' salaries or job security in any way. Accordingly, a task
force member who is not responsible for evaluating teachers'
performances coordinates the activities.

Determining the extent to which students learn decision-making
skills and take responsibility for planning, monitoring, and evaluating their own instructional and total educational programs.

A checklist for students, a checklist for teachers, and a
checklist for advisors will be administered.

Determining the extent to which students in pairs and small
groups take responsibility for planning and implementing their
classroom learning activities; ascertaining the extent to which
students take responsibility for governing their extracurricular
and student activity programs effectively.

Same checklist as above with items for these areas added.

Determining the extent to which student membership on school
committees increases.

Compare records of committee membership for this year and last
year.

Determining the extent to which punctuality and attendance
increase and discipline referrals, suspensions, and dropouts decrease; ascertaining the extent to which recognition of desired
citizenship behaviors increases.

Compare school records for this year and last year.

A report will be prepared summarizing the results of this
improvement program. The report will be prepared in such a manner
that results cannot be related to individual students or to individual teachers.

10. Refinement and Renewal

The cycle of evaluation, goal-setting, planning, and implementing improvements to attain the goals will continue on an annual
basis. Ineffective practices will be eliminated and effective
practices will be maintained and strengthened. As the staff
continues to engage in this cycle of activities and as more sophisticated staff development continues, the school will strengthen its
improvement capability and experience renewal as a social organization.

11. Time Schedule

See Chapter 1 for suggestions on developing a time schedule.

12. Budget

See Chapter 1 for suggestions on preparing a budget.

Activities Planned To Improve School Climate, 1983-84: John Burroughs Middle School, Milwaukee WI

Burroughs enrolls approximately 1,100 students in grades 7
and 8.

Introduction

At Burroughs, school discipline will emphasize a counseling
approach rather than the punishment of misbehavior. Student
misconduct will be viewed as the result not only of the student's
own misinclination but as a whole combination of environmental,
institutional, and individual causes. The role of the coordinator
of discipline will evolve from policeman to ombudsman. All
teachers will be involved in encouraging acceptable behavior on the
part of their students who will also be their advisees.

Rules governing the school environment and rules about procedures, grooming, and discipline will remain, but they will be
democratically developed by all interested parties (administration,
faculty, parents, students).

Goal: Maintain attendance at 90% or above.

Activities:

Student recognition through PA announcements.
Letters to parents.
Award to homebase for best attendance during marking period.
Orientation program for all students.
Display student pictures for perfect attendance.

Goal: Recognize students for excellent achievement.

Activities:

Picture displayed on wall in corridor.
Fieldtrip.
Luncheon.
Formal letters to parents from counselor, teachers, and principal.
Homebase teacher to display names and grade points earned.
Generate achievement reports.

Goal: Ensure security and safety of staff and students.

Activities:

Prevent outsiders from entering and loitering in building.
Schedule hall and door supervision as needed.
Post all entries with large signs stating loitering ordinance.
Encourage students not to invite relatives and friends from outside without authorization.
Maintain clean, attractive building.
Report all graffiti in restrooms and hallways to engineering staff for immediate removal.
Strengthen building security and safety for students and staff.
Purchase additional Walkie-talkie equipment identical to that used at the high schools and currently in use.

Goal: Recognize students for acts of good citizenship.

Activities:

Provide on-the-spot recognition for:
Return of lost items.
Actions of assistance of one student to another in hallways or class which is unsolicited but observed by others.

Picking up litter without being told.
Keeping school cafeteria in order after each setting.
Continue PA announcements reinforcing those who have won an award for the previous day.

Completed Project—Increasing Attendance by Use of Computer 1984-85: Wm. Horlick High School, Racine, WI

Horlick enrolls approximately 2,000 students in grades 9-12.

Persons Who Planned and Monitored the Project: Truancy task force consisting of the principal, an assistant principal, a teacher project coordinator, and a district official.

Primary Implementation Activities: Each teacher reports the absentees from each class. The absentees' names are input to the computer hourly. By means of a computer-managed calling machine, each absentee's parents are called in the evening of the same day or the next morning. They are informed of the student's absence.

In addition to initiating the calls, the computer is programmed to perform the following:

Post daily absences, which eliminates the manual use of cards.

Provide a printout of student absences, hour by hour.

Provide a printout of a dialing record which is a report of the homes that were contacted.

Provide a grid which is displayed on the monitor for reference to an individual student's record of absences.

Produce an administrative profile, which is a printout of all students and their truancy patterns by day or week, for the entire school.

This new approach has replaced the use of expensive forms, stamps, and cover letters that took hours of teacher and clerical time to prepare and three to seven days to reach parents. It has encouraged students to attend class because they know the computer knows when they miss a class. They also know that the computer will call home every time a class is missed but they do not know when it is going to call. The daily number of truancies, which are tallied hourly, has dropped by two-thirds, from a range of 588-645 to a range of 181-220. The weekly total has dropped from 2,360 to 1,050.

Chapter 7
Evaluation and Improvement Strategies:
Using Information Constructively

Rationale

Recommended Program of Testing and Other Data Gathering

Design Objectives

Preplanning Activities

Prototypic Plan

Improvement Plan—Standardized Achievement
and Mental Ability Testing, 1983-84:
Cedarburg School District, Cedarburg, WI

Rationale

Many school districts are spending large sums of money on testing but are not using the information to improve the education of either individual students or groups of students, such as all of those enrolled in middle school or high school. However, the schools of other districts are using the information very effectively in implementing each phase of the following general improvement strategy:

1. Identifying student outcomes that are already excellent and educative processes that are effective and that, therefore, are to be maintained, and identifying others that are not completely satisfactory.
2. Developing an improvement plan for each unsatisfactory area.
3. Implementing the planned improvement activities and monitoring progress carefully to ensure success.
4. Determining the extent to which the improvement activities were effective.

Norm-referenced and criterion-referenced test scores and teachers' grades and ratings may be regarded in the same way as matches. They can be used very constructively, very destructively, or not at all. Effective schools use test scores very constructively; however, some schools haven't made as much progress in using teachers' grades.

Recommended Program of Testing and Other Data Gathering

Information must be gathered on a systematic basis from year to year in order to implement the preceding general strategy. A recommended program of testing and other information gathering follows:

1. Teacher-constructed paper-and-pencil tests, performance tests, work samples, and observations for measuring student progress during the course and final achievement at the end of the course.
2. Standardized achievement tests in the academic subjects administered at least in every other grade in either the fall or the spring.

3. Criterion-referenced tests including minimum competency tests in various skill areas administered in the fall and spring of each grade.
4. Grade point average in each subject for each student and for the composite group of students of each grade.
5. A mental ability test at each school level preferably at the same time that the first standardized achievement testing is done.
6. Other measures of student outcomes in the cognitive domain, e.g., creativity, writing skills, thinking skills, etc., as desired by the school.
7. Average daily attendance (annual).
8. Incidence of discipline referrals (annual).
9. Incidence of suspensions (annual).
10. Incidence of dropouts (annual).
11. An inventory of student learning styles administered at least once at each school level.
12. An inventory or questionnaire to secure student opinion regarding learning, school, teachers, peers, and other elements of schooling, administered at least once at each school level.
13. A student self-concept inventory administered at least once at each school level.
14. Opinions of teachers, students, and parents as necessary to evaluate the effectiveness of an improvement program.

The preceding kinds of information may be used in assessing the performances and learning characteristics of individual students and group of students. However, no information should be gathered unless it will be used to facilitate student learning or to improve instructional, advising, or other schooling processes.

In this regard evaluation that is conducted without gathering and analyzing quantitative information is not to be overlooked. For example, the English teachers getting together at the end of the first grading period to share their opinions regarding how well their courses are meeting the educational needs of the students can be as useful in improving English instruction as studying the students' test scores and letter grades. Similarly, the social studies teacher may use part of the last class of the semester to secure each student's opinion of how worthwhile or how appropriate the course was for him or her.

This chapter focuses both on improving evaluation practices and on using evaluative information to improve schooling through implementing the assessment, planning, implementation, monitoring, evaluation strategy, also referred to as the goal-setting strategy, outlined in Chapter 1.

Design Objectives

Comprehensive Objectives:

A districtwide program of testing and other data gathering is maintained to ascertain the extent to which the school's program goals and the district's goals are attained annually. The individual student's progress toward attaining his or her course objectives, the student's instructional program in each course, the student's total educational program, and the school's total educational program are evaluated systematically; and the results of the evaluation are used in improving the educative processes of the school. (Evaluation is interpreted to include pre-assessment, ongoing assessment, and post-assessment.)

Illustrative Enabling Objectives:

Appropriate measurement and evaluation techniques are used in:

Monitoring each student's progress toward attaining his or her learning goals in each course and evaluating each student's instructional program toward the end of each course.

Monitoring each student's total educational program and evaluating the program toward the end of each semester.

Evaluating each student's total educational program toward the end of each school level.

Monitoring attainment of the school's improvement goals and ascertaining the extent to which goals are attained.

The results of post-evaluations are used by:

Teachers and teaching teams to arrange better instructional programs for individual students.

Advisors to arrange better total educational programs for individual students.

The school improvement committee in identifying areas for improvement and in setting related improvement goals.

The district improvement committee in identifying areas for districtwide improvement and in setting related improvement goals.

Preplanning Activities

Members of either the Educational Improvement Committee or a task force on evaluation carry out the following preplanning activities:

View and discuss the filmstrip "Evaluating Student Learning and Educational Programs in Secondary Schools."

Listen to and discuss relevant sections of the audiocassette "Experiences of a Middle School and a Senior High School with Evaluating Student Learning and Educational Programs."

Study textbook Chapter 7, "Evaluation and Improvement Strategies."

Study the materials related to individual educational programming, individual instructional programming, and curricular arrangements.

Visit schools that have effective evaluation practices, confer with other schools by phone and mail, and secure measurement instruments, test manuals, and other printed material.

Assess their school's present situation; identify improvements in evaluation practices; outline means of implementing the improvements; determine the inservice education that will be needed and whether it will be conducted by the local school staff or secured from an external source; and estimate the cost of preparing for, implementing, and continuing the improvements.

Prototypic Plan

The members of either the Educational Improvement Committee or a task force on evaluation of student learning prepare the improvement plan. Other teachers, parents, students, and other persons are invited to participate in relevant aspects of the planning process. A district official serves as an ad hoc member of the task force or as a consultant to it. The school's plan is based on the district guidelines for testing and evaluation.

1. Area of Improvement

Using assessment information in implementing the goal-based improvement strategy, with particular emphasis on goal-setting.

2. Need for Improvement

A norm-referenced educational achievement test battery is administered in April to the students of grades 7, 9, and 11. The results are examined by principals and counselors but not by teachers. The district office publishes the mean scores annually in the local newspaper. A mental ability test is administered at the same time in grades 7, 9, and 11, but the results are not used by anyone. An inventory that measures students' attitudes about schooling and their self-concepts is administered in September in grades 6, 8, and 10, but these results are not used by teachers, counselors, or students. Teacher letter grades and grade point averages in the subject fields and ratings of other student outcomes, such as writing skills, are not used regularly in planning students' educational programs or in improving instruction.

3. Percent of Students and Grades Involved

100% of the students of grades 7-12.

4. Persons Who Will Plan, Coordinate, and Evaluate the Program

The Educational Improvement Committee or the evaluation task force.

5. Persons Who Will Implement the Program

The task force members and all teachers.

6. Improvement Goals

(The use of evaluation information in implementing the individual educational programming strategy and the instructional programming strategy were presented in Chapters 2 and 3. Here the use of the available data given in [2] in setting measurable goals is illustrated. The goals assume that the school staff judges the standardized achievement test results for grades 7, 9, and 11 to reflect students' actual achievement of curriculum objectives quite reliably.)

General Goal--Mathematics

The students of each grade 8, 10, and 12 will achieve higher in mathematics, the subject field in which the mean score was lowest on the standardized test in grades 7, 9, and 11; and the grade 8, 10, and 12 students whose mathematics achievement percentile ranks were far below their mental ability percentile ranks will be aided in performing better in mathematics.

Performance Goals

The mean percentile rank of the students of grades 7, 9, and 11 will equal or exceed the 70th percentile on the standardized test, roughly equivalent to their mean percentile rank on the mental ability test.

Each student of grades 8, 10, and 12 whose achievement percentile rank in grades 7, 9, and 11 was markedly lower than his or her mental ability percentile rank will be aided in achieving higher; other students will be aided in at least maintaining their satisfactory or above level of achievement in relation to mental ability.

The grade-point average in mathematics of the students of each grade will be at or above 3.2, with 4.0 being A.

General Goal--Writing Skills

Low-achieving students of each grade 7-12 will demonstrate higher achievement in writing skills.

Performance Goals

The mean rating of each student of each grade on a writing sample will be 3.0 or higher on a 4.0 scale.

The average grade-point average of the students of each grade in writing will be 3.0 or higher with 4.0 being A.

General Goal--Student Attitudes and Self-Concepts

The attitudes of the students of all grades toward schooling and toward self will become more positive.

Performance Goals

The mean attitude ratings of the students of grades 6, 8, and 10 toward learning, school authority and control, peers, and teachers as measured by the attitude inventory will equal or exceed 3.4 on a 4.0 scale.

The mean academic self-concept rating of the students of grades 6, 8, and 10 as measured by the attitude inventory will equal or exceed 3.4 on a 4.0 scale.

The attitudes toward school and self of the students of grades 7, 9, and 11 as estimated by the teachers will be equivalent to those of the students of grades 8, 10, and 12 as measured by the attitude inventory.

7. Preparatory Activities

Arrange the teaching schedules of the task force members and provide substitute teachers as necessary so that the committee can meet during regular school hours for planning, group problem solving, and similar activities. As necessary, arrange for them to meet outside school hours to gain information and to plan.

Aid the teachers in extending their understanding of the evaluation, goal-setting, planning, and implementation sequence by leading the study of the correlated WRISE materials on evaluation, individual instructional programming, and individual educational programming; by arranging for school visits, consultants, etc.; and by examining evaluation materials used in other schools.

With respect to each of the preceding performance goals, make clear to the teachers:

What is being measured and why it is, for example, student achievement, student attitudes, teacher opinion.

How the results of the measurements of last year were used in identifying areas of improvement for the current year, setting the preceding goals, and developing related improvement plans.

How the teachers and members of the task force will use the performance goals, last year's measurements, and this year's ongoing measurements of student performance in monitoring progress during the current year.

How the results of the two successive annual measurements (tests, inventories, grade-point averages, other teacher estimates) will be used in evaluating this year's goal attainment and the effectiveness of the improvement activities.

8. First-Year Implementation Activities and Monitoring Progress

Implementation Activities

Mathematics

A task force member will:

Summarize the computer printout of the standardized test results in mathematics for each grade 7, 9, and 11 for the prior year and also the mental ability test scores.

121

Indicate to the teachers of each grade 8, 10, and 12 how much the mean mathematics achievement of each grade 7, 9, and 11 was below the mean mental ability.

Provide teachers the achievement percentile, mental ability percentile, and letter grades in mathematics for each of their students.

Interpret the measurement error of the tests to the teachers and invite each teacher to use the information in trying to get higher achievement from students whose test scores and/or grades are well below their mental ability.

Each teacher will determine the extent to which his or her judgments are in accord with the test results, indicate the judgments to the task force member, and then attempt to keep satisfactory student achievement high and raise that of low achievers.

The mathematics teachers of grades 7, 9, and 11 will implement the planned improvement activities for grades 7, 9, and 11 that are designed to raise the mean achievement of the students of these grades.

Writing Skills

The English teachers of grades 7-12 will:

Provide instruction in writing as planned.

Give a different writing assignment toward the end of each grading period.

Rate each student's performance.

Use the results to recognize and maintain students' satisfactory performances and to improve unsatisfactory performances.

Student Attitudes and Self-Concepts

(Note: Students do not enter their names on the attitude inventory to insure honesty in responding, but they do indicate their grade in school; and they may indicate the classes in which they are enrolled.) Task force members and the teachers of grades 7-12 proceed in interpreting the inventory results and in implementing the planned activities for developing more favorable student attitudes and more positive self-concepts. They follow procedures similar to those given earlier for mathematics.

122

With respect to the performance goals in mathematics, writing, attitudes toward schooling, and self-concepts:

Teachers monitor the progress of the students in their classes.

Teachers discuss their progress and concerns with one another and with a task force member.

A task force member observes the teachers' classes, examines the tests and other measurement devices the teachers construct, examines grades assigned to students, and observes group meetings of teachers for the purpose of aiding the teachers implement the improvement activities and monitor student progress. If a teacher is experiencing difficulty and desires assistance, the task force member provides it directly or has other school or district persons provide it.

9. Evaluation of the Implementation Activities

The purpose of the evaluation activities that follow, and also of the preceding monitoring, is solely to improve evaluation practices, not to arrive at judgments that influence teachers' salaries or job security in any way. Accordingly, a task force member who is not responsible for evaluating teachers' performances coordinates the activities.

Accuracy and use of standardized test scores, inventory scores, teacher ratings of students' writing, and teacher-assigned grades.

To determine accuracy, the task force performs reliability estimates for each kind of measure for each grade or for smaller subgroups of each grade, such as classes. (Universities and test publishers have computer programs that can secure these estimates very quickly and at very low cost.)

To determine how well the various measures were used to aid students learn, the task force secures opinions of teachers and students.

The task force summarizes the preceding information and recommends satisfactory measuring devices and uses of test scores to be maintained and any found unsatisfactory to be dropped, modified, or replaced.

Use of the measurement results in setting goals, planning, implementing planned activities, and monitoring progress.

The task force:

Summarizes the data its members have gathered during the year by observing classes, participating in meetings with teachers, and examining grades and ratings assigned by teachers.

Meets with groups of teachers to secure their opinions.

Combines the preceding information and proposes satisfactory practices to be maintained and others to be dropped, improved, or replaced.

Use of two consecutive sets of measurements in evaluating goal attainment, effectiveness of the planned improvement activities, and need for refinement.

The task force:

Prepares an evaluation report covering the above items, based on a comparison of the two successive measurements—mathematics, writing, and student attitude and self-concept.

Interprets the findings to groups of teachers and secures their opinions regarding possible changes or modifications.

Recommends continuing satisfactory uses and changing, modifying, or replacing any found to be unsatisfactory.

A report is prepared summarizing the results of this improvement program. The report is prepared in such a manner that results cannot be related to individual students or to individual teachers.

10. Refinement

The cycle of evaluation, goal-setting, planning, implementing improvements, and monitoring to attain the goals will continue on an annual basis. Ineffective practices will be eliminated and effective practices will be maintained and strengthened, based on the findings from [9] above.

11. Time Schedule

See Chapter 1 for suggestions on developing a time schedule.

12. Budget

See Chapter 1 for suggestions on preparing a budget.

Improvement Plan—Standardized Achievement and Mental Ability Testing, 1983-84: Cedarburg School District, Cedarburg, WI

(The Cedarburg School District includes three elementary schools, one middle school, and one high school.)

1. Area of Improvement

Standardized achievement and mental ability testing.

2. Need for Improvement

At present, three different standardized achievement tests are used. One test battery is used in grades 3 and 5; a standardized reading test only is used in middle school grades 6, 7, and 8; and a third test battery is used in high school grades 9 and 11. A mental ability test produced by the respective test publishers is administered in grades 3 and 5 and grades 9 and 11; a different mental ability test is used in grade 7.

This program of testing does not provide comparable information across the three levels of schooling that can be used effectively in assessing the achievement of individual students or groups of students in the English language arts, mathematics, science, or social studies.

3. Percent of Students and Grades Involved

100% of the students in grades 3, 5, 7, 9, and 11.

4. Persons Who Will Select and Evaluate the Tests

The District Director of Instruction, the District Test Committee, and teachers and the principal of each school.

5. Persons Who Will Use the Tests

Each school staff.

6. Improvement Goals

General Goal

The achievement test battery selected will measure student achievement in grades 3, 5, 7, 9, and 11 in language arts, mathematics, science, social studies, and work study skills (a science test is not essential at grade 3). The mental ability test selected will measure the ability of students of grades 3, 5, 7, 9, and 11 to learn the subject matter measured by the test battery.

Performance Goals

Each main test of the achievement test battery will have subtests and/or sets of items that measure the main curriculum objectives of grades 3, 5, 7, 9, and 11. While the number of items of each test may not be proportional to the amount of content actually taught, there will be at least one or two items relevant to each main curriculum objective.

The manual for the achievement battery selected will indicate high test reliability for each test and high predictive validity from one grade to the next.

The manual for the mental ability test selected will indicate high test reliability and high validity for predicting the achievement measured by each test of the achievement battery.

The tests will be easy to administer and competitive in price with similar tests.

The test publisher will score the test and return the results within a short period of time after receiving the answer sheets.

The test publisher will provide a computer printout that is easily interpreted in terms of the individual student's scores and the mean scores of groups of students.

The test publisher will provide a clear explanation of how to use the test results.

The test publisher will provide consultation regarding any aspect of the test administration and test results.

7. Preparatory Activities

The test committee will select several achievement and mental ability tests from which to choose. Examination copies will be gotten from these companies and circulated at the appropriate grade levels. Teachers of these grades will examine the various tests in light of the General and Performance Goals given in [6].

The teachers of each school will evaluate the tests in terms of acceptability, particularly in terms of the first performance goal. (The District Test Committee selected only tests that met the other criteria.) The Test Committee will receive each school's evaluations and discuss any discrepancies among the schools. The

Committee will then select an achievement test battery and a mental ability test.

After the test is selected, the consultant of the selected test company will be asked to provide appropriate inservice activities for administrators, specialists, and teachers. Areas to be included are testing students with exceptional educational needs, use of the data for district and building improvement activities, and use of the data in planning and counseling with individual students. The consultant will also provide general information regarding normative testing and relate this to the technical characteristics of the selected tests.

8. First-Year Implementation Activities

Administer the tests in the spring to each grade 3, 5, 7, 9, and 11 according to the instructions provided in the test manual.

The District Director of Instruction and principals in the summer examine the computer printouts provided by the test publisher and outline a general procedure for explaining the test results and their uses to each school staff. The high school will proceed as follows:

Test data returned in the summer will be examined by the principal and instructional coordinator to identify the academic area(s) which might need intervention in the fall. (The mastery portion of the test pertaining to the stated test objectives must be used to identify the skill areas in which students are low.) Based on the objective mastery portion of the individual student's reports, the skill areas at the non-mastery level (less than 50% correct) will be recorded, by student, on cumulative lists. These lists will be used to identify subject areas and individuals with deficiencies.

Area deficiencies will be used to formulate improvement plans in content areas, e.g., English or mathematics. Individual deficiencies will be recorded and used for instructional intervention purposes and for teacher/advisor, parent, and student conferences. The conference will involve explaining the test results to the parents in terms of real and expected achievement as well as local and national percentile rankings.

To prepare for this detailed explanation of the test and its uses, the teacher/advisors will meet with the instructional coordinator several times during the month which precedes the fall advisement conferences. After initially reviewing the test, the teacher/ advisor will take part in a role-playing exercise in which he or she will explain the test results to other teacher/advisors playing the roles of parents. This exercise can be done with actual advisees' interpretive reports by using an opaque projector.

9. Evaluation of the Tests and Uses of the Test Results

Each school will evaluate how well the achievement test battery measured the main curriculum objectives and how well the mental ability test estimated the ability of the students to learn the content measured by the test. Each school will also evaluate how well the test results are being used in the improvement of instruction and advising. To illustrate, the high school instructional coordinator will secure teachers' opinions regarding the characteristics of the tests. The high school Academic Improvement Committee will prepare and administer teacher, parent, and student questionnaires to evaluate the effectiveness of the uses being made of the test results.

10. Refinement

After the first-year evaluation, a decision will be made about whether the commitment of further time and resources is timely and purposeful.

11. Time Schedule

	Starting Data	Ending Date
Preparatory activities	Fall 1982	Spring 1983
First-year implementation	Spring 1983	Spring 1984
First-year evaluation	Spring 1983	Spring 1984
Refinement	1984-85	1985-87

12. Budget

$1,500 - Test Materials.

Chapter 8
Organizing Students and Teachers for Instruction: It's Time To Replace 19th Century Patterns

Rationale

Organizational Patterns

Benefits of Teaming

Design Objectives

Preplanning Activities

Prototypic Plan

Rationale

How teachers and students are organized for instruction and advising greatly affects the frequency and the constructiveness of the communications among the school staff. In sensibly organized schools, the chronic complaining in the teachers' lounge about students, parents, low pay, and intolerable working conditions had been replaced with constructive communication and cooperative small-group problem solving. Even more important, the impersonality of typical teacher-student and home-school communications is changed to personalized, caring interactions. In making these changes, schools depart from the departmental organization and counselors being responsible for all advising.

This chapter focuses on the organization of teachers and students for instruction. Chapter 9 presents information regarding teacher-advising.

Organizational Patterns

In many middle schools the academic teachers and students are organized into instructional and advisory units. Each unit has three to five academic teachers and 75 to 125 students. A special education teacher and special education students are often part of an academic unit. The foreign language, allied arts, and other teachers are also organized into teams but they teach all the students rather than a particular group of students.

In this organizational pattern, the academic teachers have the students for a block of time equivalent to about two-thirds of the time that is allocated daily for instruction. The team teaches the students English, mathematics, reading, science, and social studies. The teachers also serve formally or informally as educational advisors to 15 to 25 students of the unit, and one or more allied arts and other teachers also advise some of the students of each unit.

Some high schools follow the middle school interdisciplinary pattern with respect to their organization for instruction, particularly in grades 9 and 10 if all or most of the students of these grades take English, mathematics, science, and social studies. Other high schools organize their teachers and students into disciplinary units. In Milwaukee high schools, each having one to three career specialty programs such as computer technology or health services, teams with as many as 10 members provide all

131

the required academic and specialty courses to 200 or more students of grades 11 and 12 enrolled in the specialty program. Essentially, this career specialty program is a school within the larger school. Some small alternative high schools have the entire teaching staff organized into an instructional team. Two-teacher interdisciplinary teams are also common, such as English and social studies or mathematics and science.

Figure 8.1 shows how the school day is organized into approximate blocks of time when groups of students and interdisciplinary teams of English, mathematics, science, and social studies teachers are organized into units in either the middle school or the high school. Although the difference is not shown in Figure 8.1, about two-thirds of the middle school day and half of the high school day typically is allocated to the four required subjects. Also not apparent is the fact that there are fewer required subjects and more electives in grades 11 and 12 than in grades 9 and 10.

Benefits of Teaming

We see that with teaming and scheduling as shown in Figure 8.1, some time is available daily for each academic team to meet together for planning and other activities. Also, time can be arranged weekly for the Educational Improvement Committee to meet, including a representative of each team.

There are many benefits from organizing academic teachers and students into small instructional units. It facilitates the establishment of an effectively functioning educational improvement committee. This time arrangement also enables the principal to exercise the effective educational leadership that he or she is capable of. The principal involves all the teachers in the improvement process since a block of time is available daily during regular school hours for cooperative preparation, planning, and other activities by groups of teachers with mutual improvement interests. If the teachers also serve as advisors to the students, this organization makes it possible for the school to gain parental support as each teacher establishes and maintains good working relationships with the parents of his or her advisees (see Chapter 9). Since the academic teams have a block of time during each school day, district office persons as well as the school's learning coordinator, principal, resource teachers, and others can provide many types of support to the teams in small groups, rather than having to reach individual teachers outside of the regular school day.

7:30

```
                    INSTRUCTIONAL CONFERENCE AND PLANNING BLOCK
· · · · · · · · · · ·|· · · · · · · · · ·|· · · · · · · · ·|· · · · · · · ·
                     Other required or
                     elective courses,
                     study periods,      Other required or
                     extracurricular     elective courses,
                     activities, etc.    study periods,     Other required or
                     · · · · · · · ·     extracurricular    elective courses,
                                         activities, etc.   study periods,
                                                            extracurricular
  Interdisciplinary                                         activities, etc.
  Instructional
  Block  A                              · · · · · · · ·


                     Interdisciplinary                     · · · · · · · ·
                     Instructional
                     Block B

                                         Interdisciplinary
  · · · · · · · ·                         Instructional
                                         Block C

                                                            Interdisciplinary
                                                            Instructional
  Other required or   · · · · · · · ·                       Block D
  elective courses,
  study periods,
  extracurricular     Other required or
  activities, etc.    elective courses,  · · · · · · · ·
                      study periods,
                      extracurricular    Other required or
                      activities, etc.   elective courses,
                                         study periods,
                                         extracurricular
  · · · · · · · ·  |· · · · · · · ·  |· · · · · · · · ·  activities, etc.
                                                       |· · · · · · · ·
                    INSTRUCTIONAL CONFERENCE AND PLANNING BLOCK
```

3:30

Figure 8.1. General time schedule for secondary schools where about
120 students and English, mathematics, science, and
social studies teachers are organized into instructional
units. Depending on the enrollment of the school, lunch
is for one to three short periods.

133

Related to the implementation of the three improvement strategies, this organization makes it possible for each academic team to participate directly in the implementation of the goal-based improvement strategy:

Identify areas of improvement for individual students and the entire group of students of the unit.

Set realistic goals and develop plans to achieve the goals.

Implement the planned activities.

Monitor each student's progress.

Evaluate the effectiveness of the improvement activities.

The teacher advisor is able to implement the individual educational programming strategy:

Plan the total educational program of each student of the unit with the student and parents.

Monitor the student's progress systematically at three-week intervals or more often.

Evaluate the appropriateness and value of the program for the student toward the end of the year.

Similarly, each teacher is able to implement the individual instructional programming strategy with each student enrolled in each of his or her courses:

Plan an instructional program with each student.

Implement the program and monitor the student's progress.

Evaluate the appropriateness and value of the program for the student.

Design Objectives

Comprehensive Objective

The faculty and students are organized into small groups that permit instruction and advising to be personalized.

<u>Illustrative Enabling Objectives</u>

A teacher of each instructional group:

Chairs the meetings of the group.

Serves on the school's Educational Improvement Committee and participates in the Committee's planning and other activities.

Transmits information, decisions, and plans from the teaching staff to the Educational Improvement Committee.

Transmits information, decisions, and plans to the teaching staff.

Related to instruction, each group of teachers, such as an interdisciplinary teaching team, cooperatively:

Develops the procedures for planning, monitoring, and evaluating each student's instructional program in each course taught by the group.

Plans and evaluates the group's instructional strategies.

Related to the group's instructional functions, each teacher:

Outlines the content of his or her courses.

Develops the learning guides that students use in the courses.

Plans the instructional methods that are employed in the courses, including the use of time, materials, and modes of instruction.

Participates in all aspects of the group's planning and evaluation activities.

Carries out his or her instructional activities in accordance with the group's plans.

Preplanning Activities

The members of either the Educational Improvement Committee or a task force on organization for instruction lead the preplanning and prepare the improvement plan. Other teachers, parents, students, and other persons are invited to participate in relevant aspects of the planning process. A district official serves as an ad hoc member of the task force or as a consultant to it. The school's plan is based on the district's planning guidelines.

Study textbook Chapter 9, "Organization for Instruction and Student Advising."

View and discuss the filmstrip "Instruction and Advisory Arrangements in Secondary Schools."

Listen to and discuss relevant sections of the audiocassette "Experiences of Two Middle Schools and Two Senior High Schools with Instruction and Advisory Arrangements."

Study the closely related materials on "Teacher-Advisor Programs," "Educational Programming for the Individual Student," "Instructional Programming for the Individual Student," and "Administrative Arrangements and Processes."

Visit schools that have desired organizational arrangements, confer with other schools by phone and mail, and secure descriptions of effectively functioning organizations.

Assess the school's present organization for instruction, identify how changes in the organization will contribute to improving the school's educative processes, outline possible means of implementing the changes, determine the kind of inservice education that will be needed and whether it will be conducted by the local staff or secured from an external source, and estimate the costs of preparing for and implementing the changed organization for instruction.

Develop an awareness program to gain faculty, parent, and student understanding and support for changing to the new organization for instruction.

Prototypic Plan

1. Area of Improvement

   Organization for Instruction.

2. Need for Improvement

   A teacher task force found that the present departmentalized organization for instruction isolates teachers from one another and inhibits interdisciplinary cooperation among teachers. It also discourages planning a well-balanced educational program for each student and monitoring the student's progress. It promotes impersonal relations between teachers and their students, resulting in some teachers failing many students and encouraging them to withdraw from the class or even from school.

3. Percent of Students and Grades Involved

100% of the students.

4. Persons Who Will Plan, Coordinate, and Evaluate the Program

The Educational Improvement Committee or task force on organizing for instruction.

5. Persons Who Will Implement the Program

All teachers, counselors, and administrators.

6. Improvement Goals

General Goal--Instructional Improvement

Each student taught by a team member will receive excellent instruction.

Performance Goals

The number of teachers implementing the individual instructional programming strategy effectively will increase from 0 to the total number of teachers of each team (see Chapter 4).

The number of students who attain most of their learning goals will increase from 50% to 80%.

General Goal--Communication

Communication and cooperation among teachers, and also among teachers, administrators, and other school staff will increase.

Performance Goals

During a typical school week, the amount of time that members of each team engage in constructive face-to-face communication with other teachers will increase from two to six hours.

During any given month of school, the amount of time that at least one member of each team engages in constructive face-to-face communication with a member of the administrative team and with some other teachers, counselors, and other certificated staff of the school will increase from 30 minutes to two hours.

General Goal--Improvement Capability

The school's improvement capability will be strengthened.

Performance Goals

During a typical week and without an increase in the hours of work, the amount of time that each teacher spends on improvement activities will increase from 0 to 5 hours.

During a typical month and without a decrease in contact hours with students, the amount of time that representative teachers on the EIC spend on schoolwide improvement activities will increase from 0 to 4 hours.

The mean rating of teachers' job satisfaction will increase from 7.5 to 8.5 on a 10-point scale.

7. Preparatory Activities

Arrange the teaching schedules of the task force members and provide substitute teachers as necessary so that the planning group can meet during regular school hours. As necessary, arrange for the planning group to meet outside school hours to gain information and to plan.

Assist the school staff in preparing to implement the organization for instruction by leading the study of the correlated WRISE materials used earlier as a preplanning activity, by arranging for the staff to visit schools that have exemplary practices, by making available descriptive materials from schools with exemplary practices, and, if necessary, by arranging for consultants to conduct inservice activities.

Carry out an awareness-commitment program with students, parents, and other citizens to ensure that the proposed organization is understood and supported.

8. First-Year Implementation Activities and Monitoring Progress

Implementation Activities

Instructional Improvement

Each team of teachers meets regularly to:

Share progress and effective practices.

Solve instructional problems cooperatively.

Facilitate each teacher's implementation of the individual instructional programming strategy.

Monitor each student's progress in each course taught by the teacher.

Participate in staff development activities arranged by the school or the district office.

Communication

Each interdisciplinary or disciplinary team of teachers:

Meets at least three hours weekly to discuss progress and concerns, plan, prepare for instruction, and participate in staff development activities conducted by a staff member outside the team.

Meets with school or district office persons for the equivalent of at least one hour weekly to exchange information and to engage in staff development activities directed toward the improvement of schooling.

Improvement Capability

Each team meets regularly for the purpose of contributing to schoolwide improvement activities that relate to their instructional group.

A teacher representative of each team participates in the meeting of the Educational Improvement Committee, transmits information from the team to the Committee and from the Committee to the team, and performs other Committee work. One or more teachers of the team serve on relevant improvement task forces.

Monitoring Progress

A task force member will periodically interview selected teachers, counselors, students, and parents to determine their perceptions regarding the effectiveness of the new organization for instruction. These individuals will indicate acute unresolved problems, if any, and the task force member or a school or district person will provide immediate assistance in resolving the problems.

9. Evaluation of the Implementation Activities

The purpose of the evaluation activities that follow, and also of the preceding monitoring activities, is solely to strengthen the school's organization for instruction, not to arrive at judgments that influence teachers' or administrators' salaries or job security in any way. Accordingly, a task force member who is not responsible for evaluating staff performances coordinates the evaluation activities.

Instructional Improvement

In May administer a questionnaire, not to be signed, that has items to ascertain for last year and this year whether the teacher (a) planned an instructional program with each student, (b) monitored each student's progress in each course, and (c) evaluated the appropriateness of each student's instructional program in each course. Include another item to get the teacher's estimate of the number of his or her students who attained their learning goals.

Interview a sample of the teachers and students if time permits.

Communication

Include items in the preceding questionnaire that call for teachers to indicate for last year and this year the number of minutes spent individually and/or in small-group meetings working with (a) other teachers and (b) administrators, counselors, and other staff on school matters that the teacher regards as significant, not on managerial concerns such as distributing materials, getting grades out, and scheduling field trips.

If time permits, interview a sample of the teachers to secure more detailed information.

Improvement Capability

Include an item in the prior questionnaire to ascertain the number of minutes that the teacher last year and this year spent on schoolwide improvement activities, including the implementation of the new organization for instruction.

Include an item in the prior questionnaire to get at job satisfaction; have a 1 rating mean highly dissatisfied and 10 highly satisfied.

As time permits, interview a sample of the teachers.

A report is prepared summarizing the results from implementing the organization for instruction.

10. Refinement and Renewal

The cycle of evaluation, goal setting, planning, and implementation will continue on an annual basis. Ineffective practices and activities will be discontinued, while effective practices and activities will be maintained and strengthened. As the staff continues to engage in this cycle of activities and as more sophisticated staff development continues, the school will refine its improvement capability and will experience renewal as a social organization.

11. Time Schedule

See Chapter 1 for suggestions on developing a time schedule.

12. Budget

See Chapter 1 for suggestions on preparing a budget.

Chapter 9
Personalizing Educational Advising:
How To Combat the 250:1 Ratio

Rationale

Ways of Implementing Teacher-Advisor Programs

Determining Whether To Start a Teacher-Advisor Program

Design Objectives

Preplanning Activities

Preparing To Start a Teacher-Advisor Program, 1983-84:
Parkview High School, Orfordville, WI

Basic Considerations When Planning and Starting
a Teacher-Advisor Program, 1982-83:
Cedarburg High School, Cedarburg, WI

Improvement Plan—
Starting a Teacher-Advisor Program, 1984-85:
Ashwaubenon High School, Green Bay, WI

Improvement Plan—
Refinement of the Teacher-Advisor Program, 1983-85:
Webster Transitional School, Cedarburg, WI

Completed Project—
Increasing Teacher-Student Communication, 1984-85:
Franklin High School, Franklin, WI

Rationale

Professor John Rothney of UW-Madison studied dropouts of the 1950s. He found that the dropouts, almost without exception, were filled with remorse that they had not graduated. He asked them what might have prevented their dropping out. Almost without exception the dropouts said that they would not have quit school if there had been one person in high school—a teacher, a counselor, anybody—who had shown interest in them, encouraged them to continue, and given them help when they most needed it before quitting.

More recently, Harold Shane of Indiana University reported the results of his interviews with students of the 1970s regarding what they thought would improve secondary schooling. The students made two suggestions repeatedly. First, they recommended personalized, caring guidance that would help them build inner security and the ability to cope with a harsh and often frightening social world as represented in their home situations, neighborhoods, and more broadly in national and international affairs. The second recommendation was better preparation for satisfying and useful lives as adults. Caring, coping, and more open communication between students and teachers—these were the three big recurrent ideas coming from the students.

The typical counselor cannot provide the needed personalized guidance to each student because he or she has far too many student advisees. However, some schools have established teacher-advisor programs in which, working together, the counselors and teacher advisors meet most students' educational, social, and personal needs.

Ways of Implementing Teacher-Advisor Programs

Teacher advising is implemented in many different ways. In some schools four teachers of English, mathematics, science, and social studies and about 120 students are organized into an instruction and advisory unit. Each teacher serves formally or informally as an advisor to part of the students and does most of the individual conferring and small-group guidance during the block of time allocated to instruction and advising. In other schools the students are not organized into units. In these situations, (a) teachers of an interdisciplinary team serve as advisors to the students of each grade, (b) teachers of an interdisciplinary team serve as advisors to a group of students from all grades, or

(c) there is no teaming and individual teachers serve as advisors. Some schools have modified and extended their homeroom arrangements to include teacher advising; others have replaced most of the homeroom activities with individual conferences and small-group advising activities.

Determining Whether To Start
a Teacher-Advisor Program

When deciding whether to start teacher advising, eight basic issues must be addressed:

1. How much planning of the program and preparation of the staff are required?
2. What will be the role of the counselors in planning and implementing the teacher-advisor program?
3. Which grade levels will be included in each advisor group?
4. How will students be selected for each advisor group?
5. Which staff members will serve as advisors?
6. When, how often, and for how long will the advisor and his or her advisees meet as a group in a homeroom or other setting?
7. How much staff time will be required for advising?
8. How much will implementation of the program cost?

No two schools seem to resolve the preceding issues in the same way. A very large difference is found on the last two issues. In some schools no additional teacher time but some change in teacher duties is required for advising; in other schools as much time as the equivalent of a daily class period is given for advising. When no additional time is required, the cost of implementation is negligible. On the other hand, the cost is considerable when the teacher-advisors' teaching load is reduced by the equivalent of a class period.

Most schools fall between the extremes of no additional time and a daily class period required for advising. How much time is needed depends on the comprehensiveness of the advising process. It is not very time consuming to plan a student's total educational program once or twice a year, particularly if most of the information about curricular and extracurricular offerings can be provided to small groups. It is very time consuming, however, to conduct six individual conferences with each of 25 advisees and to carry out a comprehensive program of group guidance activities.

Design Objectives

Comprehensive Objective

The faculty and students are organized into small groups that permit advising to be personalized.

Illustrative Enabling Objectives

Each team of teachers implements the first advisement activity that follows and it may implement any or all of the other three:

Promoting the educational development of each student.

Enhancing the personal and social development of each student.

Improving schoolwide communication.

Improving home-school-community relations.

Each teacher of the team, with the assistance of a guidance counselor:

Serves as an advisor to a group of students.

Assumes responsibility for planning, monitoring, and evaluating each advisee's educational program and for attaining any other objectives of the advising program assumed by the team.

Preplanning Activities

Either the members of the Educational Improvement Committee or a task force on arranging an appropriate instructional program for each student carry out preplanning activities such as the following:

View and discuss the filmstrip "Teacher-Advisor Programs in Secondary Schools."

Listen to and discuss relevant sections of the audiocassette "Experiences of a Middle School and a Junior High School with Teacher-Advisor Programs, and Experiences of Two Senior High Schools with Teacher-Advisor Programs."

Read textbook Chapter 10, "Teacher-Advisor Programs."

Study the filmstrip and other correlated materials related to individual educational programming, curricular arrangements, and student decision making.

Visit schools that have teacher-advisor programs, confer with other schools by phone and mail, and secure printed material on teacher-advising.

Assess their school's present situation, identify possible improvements in advising and counseling, outline possible means of implementing a teacher-advisor program, determine the inservice education that will be needed and whether it will be conducted by the school staff or secured from an external source, and estimate the costs of planning, preparation, and implementation.

Gain faculty and parent commitment to implementing a teacher-advisor program.

Preparing To Start a Teacher-Advisor Program, 1983-84: Parkview High School, Orfordville, WI

Parkview High School enrolls 684 students in grades 7-12.

Persons Who Planned and Monitored the Project: Parkview Improvement Council consisting of the principal, one counselor, and five teachers.

Goal: To determine feasibility of starting a teacher-advisor program and, if feasible, to prepare for starting it.

Primary Implementation Activities: Our superintendent encouraged us to get involved in the WRISE program. So the principal, our two counselors, and four faculty members attended the October WRISE workshop in Lake Geneva. We were very impressed with the school improvement experiences of the practitioner staff of the workshop and the results of the advisor/advisee programs in their schools.

After the workshop, the Parkview Improvement Council visited the Cedarburg School System. We were so impressed with the impact and results of their advisor/advisee program that approximately half of our 7-12 faculty have spent a school day visiting their middle school and high school. Our superintendent as well as four of seven school board members also spent a day visiting Cedarburg.

For staff development, we have shown our faculty the WRISE filmstrip on advisement. We also delayed school one morning and had the coordinator for the Cedarburg advisor/advisee program meet with our 7-12 faculty to explain how this program works and to answer questions.

After visiting Cedarburg, the Parkview Improvement Council surveyed the faculty and the school board for goal setting. The survey focused on student academic and behavior improvements for next year and over the next five-year period. We found that the immediate (next year) and long term (next five years) student improvement goals from the faculty and the school board paralleled one another. The faculty and school board also recognize now that most of our improvement goals can be attained through a well-structured student advisement program.

We now have a unified effort for a 7-12 student advisement program and are planning for phasing in advisement starting with the 1985-86 school year.

Parkview Goal Setting Survey

Survey directions:

The Parkview Improvement Council would like to have your help in setting some short-term and long-term goals for students. Below is a list of goals. We would like to have you respond by indicating what you feel is an attainable percentage rate for each item within one year and within five years. Next, please select the three goals you feel need our more immediate attention by circling their item numbers.

Responses of School Board Members (B) and Teachers (T)

N CIRCLING		ITEM	PARKVIEW PRESENT RATE	GOAL FOR NEXT YEAR		GOAL FOR 5 YEARS FROM NOW	
B	T			B	T	B	T
3	9	1. Graduates continuing education (Voc/Tech)	25.0%	29.0%	32.0%	41.0%	40.0%
		Completion record	90.0%	91.0%	92.0%	93.0%	94.0%
1	11	2. Graduates continuing education (College)	33.0%	38.0%	37.0%	47.0%	44.0%
		Completion record	50.0%	62.0%	60.0%	80.0%	70.0%
0	2	3. CTBS Achievement Score	59	61.3	64	68	71
0	4	4. 1984 ACT Composite Scores (Wis. State Average 20.4; maximum possible score 33)	19.3	20.2	20.2	22.5	22
6	20	5. Student failure semester rate (1 or more classes)	24.0%	18.0%	19.0%	12.0%	14.0%
1	2	6. Dropout rate	2.6.%	2.3%	2.1%	1.8%	1.6%
1	18	7. Parent/teacher conference attendance	37.0%	47.0%	52.0%	84.0%	74.0%
0	0	8. Student daily attendance	94.4.%	94.8%	95.3%	95.5%	96.6%
2	10	9. Student discipline referrals/semester	832	750	674	530	506
0	5	10. Student suspensions/ semester	93	79	75	41	53

N CIRCLING		ITEM	B	T			
4	2	11. Gifted and talented program	67%	78%	Improvement needed		
			33%	22%	Okay as is		
3	15	12. Student pride and attitude	83%	100%	Improvement needed		
			17%	0%	Okay as is		

Basic Considerations When Planning and Starting a Teacher-Advisor Program, 1982-83: Cedarburg High School, Cedarburg, WI

(Enrollment 1,117 in grades 9-12 in 1982-83.)

Comment: Only the most important considerations follow in outline form and only the individual conference schedule for grade 9 advisees is given.

Preplanning, Planning, and Start-Up Activities

Clarify and articulate the district and school educational philosophy.

Establish a teacher-advisor committee consisting of representative students, counselors, teachers, and others; the committee reviews relevant literature, visits schools which have such programs, and synthesizes the information.

Assess staff and student needs.

Relate present homeroom program to proposed teacher-advisor program.

Develop the plan and submit it for approval by the entire staff.

Conduct staff development activities.

Plan strategies and develop materials necessary for the program.

Allocate adequate staff time for advising.

Implement the program.

Evaluate progress annually and make adjustments where necessary.

Advisor-Advisee Considerations

Form the advisor groups.

Determine the frequency and length of the group meetings and the meeting schedule.

Decide who will serve as the advisor of each group and of each student of each group.

Teacher-Advisors' Duties and Procedures

Advisors are responsible for planning each advisee's educational program for the ensuing year in the second semester of the current year (see Chapter 3 of this Guide), monitoring the advisee's progress in each course during the current year, and encouraging positive advisee attitudes toward schooling, including the advising process.

Long-Range Educational Programming and Goal Setting

Long-range goal setting involves identifying appropriate curricular and extracurricular offerings for all the high school years, taking into account the advisee's general interests, career interests, and learning characteristics. Advisors are responsible for working with the counselor, advisee, and parents in helping the advisee set long-range goals in terms of identifying courses and extracurricular activities for the remainder of the high school years and specifying how well the student will achieve in each one. The advisor will:

Meet with the counselor to identify the long-range goals of the advisee.

Meet with the advisee concerning long-range goals and provide needed assistance in trying to reach these goals.

Meet with the parents concerning long-range goals as they are perceived by the advisee and the parents.

Monitoring Student Achievement and Attitudes

Advisors are responsible for:

Monitoring each advisee's achievement, based on teacher referrals to the teacher-advisor, use of teachers' midquarter narrative report regarding each student, advisee self-referral, and parent referral. (Parents are encouraged to make initial contact with a counselor.)

Monitoring each advisee's attendance and providing homework when the parents request it.

Holding at least six individual conferences with each advisee annually.

Regularly Scheduled Advisor-Advisee-Parent Conferences in Grade 9

1. First Advisor-Advisee Conference (September).

   Discuss the advisee's educational program for current semester.

   Discuss advisor's, counselor's, parent's, and advisee's roles in advisor-advisee-parent conferences.

   Discuss extracurricular opportunities.

   Set advisee's achievement goals for each course in light of information supplied by middle school. (The advisee sets goals for each course in terms of the midquarter grade, quarter grade, and semester grade that he or she will make. The goals can be changed in subsequent conferences.)

   Follow-up: Enter additional biographical data in the advisee's folder.

   Contact the advisee's parent(s) by phone and briefly outline the roles of the advisor, counselor, parent, and advisee.

2. First Pre-parent Conference with Advisee (midquarter).

   Review advisee's achievement (midquarter grades and teachers' narrative reports) as close to conference as possible and compare them with the advisee's achievement goals.

   Discuss advisee's work samples.

   Discuss advisee's study habits. Discuss possible failures and necessity for make-up.

   Discuss advisee's interests, hobbies, potential career interests, etc. (See Student Information Sheet.)

   Preview parent conference and outline advisee's responsibility during that conference. (See Student Responsibility Sheet.)

3. First Advisor-Advisee-Parent Conference.

   Review advisee achievement and how it relates to achievement goals using report sheets and up-to-date teacher reports. Discuss final exams coming at end of semester.

   Explain computerized grade cards.

   Clarify role of advisor and counselor in planning student's educational program for next year.

Discuss grade 10 course offerings and how they relate to the advisee's high school plans.

Discuss nature of sophomore conference (see 4). Stress present achievement as indicator of future performance, also sophomore year as a year for more electives.

Go over graduation requirements and credit load of advisee, using course offering sheets. Give copy to parents.

4. Advisee Conference To Outline Grade 10 Educational Program (late January, February).

   Review options and obtain recommendations from advisee's counselor.

   Obtain recommendations from English and math teachers.

   Advisor-Advisee Conference

   Begin discussion of long-range goals.

   Using information gathered from counselor, teachers, students, and parents, discuss grade 10 schedule and write down tentative educational program. Signatures required.

   Review advisee's semester grades and narrative reports, compare accomplishments with achievement goals.

5. Midquarter Conference.

   Review advisee achievement and how it relates to achievement goals.

   Review grade 10 course selections and rationale for these choices.

   Discuss grade 9 standardized achievement test results.

   Preview parent conference. Review student responsibilities.

6. Second Advisor-Advisee-Parent Conference (April, before spring break).

   Review advisee's achievements and compare them with advisee's achievement goals using report sheets and up-to-date teacher reports.

   Review proposed grade 10 educational program and relate it to long-range goals.

Discuss upcoming grade 9 standardized achievement test. Present information regarding the test and the student interpretive report, and indicate that the results will be discussed again in detail in first conference next fall).

Preview upcoming General Aptitude Test Battery and describe how the results will be used in conferring about a career and working out long-range goals.

Enter a summary of each conference in the student's cumulative folder immediately after each conference.

Improvement Plan—
Starting a Teacher-Advisor Program, 1984-85:
Ashwaubenon High School, Green Bay, WI

(Enrollment 1,093 in grades 9-12 in 1983-84.)

1. Area of Improvement

Student Advising.

2. Need for Improvement

An assessment by a teacher-advisor committee showed that the school's counselors have sufficient time to schedule students' classes, confer with some students experiencing academic failure and acute personal and social problems, and confer with most students regarding career planning. They do not have time to plan each advisee's educational program in one or more individual conferences, monitor each advisee's progress, and evaluate the appropriateness and worthwhileness of each advisee's educational program.

3. Percentage of Students and Grades Involved

100% of freshmen in the 1985-86 school year.

4. Persons Who Planned and Will Coordinate and Evaluate the Program (First Year)

T-A Council consisting of the assistant principal, one counselor, and a teacher representative from each of three newly formed interdisciplinary multigrade units. (Each unit has a T-A as chairperson, one counselor, and four T-As from each grade 9-12, a total of 18 members.)

5. Persons Who Will Implement the Program

   All grade 9 teacher-advisors and counselors. (See information that follows after the Budget regarding Teacher-Advisor and Counselor duties.)

6. Improvement Goals

   All students will be assisted in:

   Realization and discovery of their potential.

   Achieving high in relation to ability as reflected in their grades.

   Developing a good educational program with less direction from a T-A or a counselor.

7. Preparatory Activities

   Carry out inservice/staff development activities starting in February 1985.

   Develop the forms necessary for the operation of the program by September 1985 through a summer writing project.

   Develop a strategy to evaluate the T-A program prior to its introduction in September 1985.

8. First-Year Implementation Activities and Monitoring Progress

   Set up support groups to aid in the sharing of ideas and assisting in the dissemination of information to the grade 9 T-As, the students, and their parents.

   Conduct inservice/staff development activities.

9. Evaluation of Implementation Activities in Terms of Goal Attainment

   For all three goals in (6), administer questionnaires to the grade 9 T-As; other grade 9 teachers, students, and parents; and the administrative team.

   Student Achievement

   Compare individual grade 9 students' letter grades and grade-point average in each subject field from one grading period to the next.

Students' Educational Program

From one semester to the next, compare the educational programs of all the grade 9 students, or a representative group of
high, average, and low achieving girls and an equal sample of boys.

Determine how many grade 9 students' educational programs were
better, equally good, and poorer, taking into account (a) each
student's educational needs and goals and (b) each student's
learning characteristics.

10. Refinement and Renewal

Refinement of the program will be ongoing while the program is
being extended from 1986-87 through 1988-89 to the students of the
successively higher grades.

11. Time Schedule

	Starting Date	Ending Date
Preplanning	October 1984	November 1984
Planning	November 1984	February 1985
Inservice Activities	February 1985	May 1986
Baseline Year Evaluation	1984-1985	1984-1985
First-Year Grade 9		
Implementation	1985-1986	1985-1986
Evaluation of First-Year		
Implementation	1985-1986	1985-1986
Implementation of Grade 10		
T-A Program	1986-1987	1986-1987
Implementation of Grade 11		
T-A Program	1987-1988	1987-1988
Implementation of Grade 12		
T-A Program	1988-1989	1988-1989

12. Budget

1984-1985	Planning, materials development, and inservice	$2,750
1985-1986	Planning, materials development, amd inservice	$4,000
1986-1989	(Budgets for each successive year to be prepared annually.)	

Counselor Duties Relative to Grade 9 Students

Continuing duties:

Provide crisis-oriented counseling to help modify the behavior of a student beginning to disfunction in school.

Gain more diagnostic information for students who have special needs.

Provide guidance to those students interested in post-high school careers or schooling.

Leadership as a member of one of the three newly formed T-A groups:

Help facilitate T-A group interactions and productivity in the group's meetings.

Work with T-As as a group during a common planning time as deemed necessary to aid them in developing or refining individual-conferencing and small-group guidance activities.

New activities:

Plan small-group guidance activities with input from T-As.

Act on referrals from staff, parents, administrators, T-As, and outside agencies.

Assist T-As in registration and schedule changes.

Provide on-the-spot assistance to the T-A regarding T-A functions.

Provide on-going communication between T-A and counselor.

Participate in student-parent-teacher conferences when necessary.

Teacher-Advisor Duties Relative to Grade 9 Students

Hold individual conferences with advisees a minimum of four times per year during school hours when both have free time, after school, or in the evening.

Monitor the academic progress of the advisee and inform advisee and parent/guardian if problems arise. Advisors will also help to find a solution to the problem if possible.

Be a contact person for the advisee and his or her parent or guardian to communicate about school and other concerns as they arise.

Help each advisee plan his or her program of course work to match the advisee's interests and vocational goals and talents.

Develop a file folder for each advisee consisting of:

Student information sheet.

Student records.

Student's four-year program (actual and projected).

Reports of conferences.

Miscellaneous reports and information as needed and collected from various sources.

Annual Allotment of Teacher-Advisor's Time
for Serving as an Advisor to 20 Students

		Total Hours
Individual conferences with each advisee	2 per quarter, 30 min. per session spread over year	80
T-A student monitoring (communication with teachers about advisees)		32
Conducting T-A related homeroom meetings	9 per quarter, 15 min. each	9
Conducting other homeroom meetings	10 per year, 15 min. each	2
Report card pick-up by parents	2 per year, 2 hours per quarter	8

(continued)

		Total Hours
T-A Program meetings per year	1 per quarter, 30 min. each	2
T-A/Parent/Student Individual Conferences	2 per year, 20 min. each	20
T-A Coordinator/Teacher Conferences	2 per quarter, 30 min. each	4
Recording and preparing reports	3 hours per quarter	12
TOTAL for year		169

Improvement Plan—
Refinement of the Teacher-Advisor Program, 1983-85:
Webster Transitional School, Cedarburg, WI

(Enrollment 652 in grades 6-8 in 1983-84.)

1. Area of Improvement

   Refinement of the Teacher-Advisor Program.

2. Need for Improvement

   A needs identification conducted by the Faculty Advisory Council (Educational Improvement Committee) indicated that the teacher-advisor program was functioning reasonably well with respect to educational advisement and home-school cooperation. However, it was not functioning as well as it had in the past in terms of desired student outcomes in the affective domain or desired teacher enthusiasm.

3. Percent of Students and Grades Involved

   100% of all students.

4. Persons Who Planned and Will Coordinate and Evaluate the Program

   The school's Faculty Advisory Council consisting of the principal, instructional coordinator, dean of students, two counselors, ten teacher representatives (one from each academic team, two from the fine arts and applied arts team), and the IMC director. (The students and academic teachers are organized into instructional and advisory units.)

5. Persons Who Will Implement the Program

All teacher advisors and counselors.

6. Improvement Goals

General Goal--Advisors

More advisors will have clearly stated objectives and long-range goals for conducting the activities of their advisees as a group.

Performance Goal--Advisors

All of the academic teams will make use of the group-advisee activities for encouraging students' social and emotional development and will allocate time to advisement to ensure continuity in their advisement throughout the school year. The advisors of each academic team will adhere to 95% or more of the plans developed by their team.

General Goal--Students

Students will understand the goals of the program and feel that the goals relative to their attitudes toward schooling, their peers, and themselves have been attained.

Performance Goal--Students

The students of each academic team will show an average increase of .5 (on a scale from 1 to 4) on the School Sentiment Index.

7. Preparatory (Staff Development/Inservice) Activities

The Faculty Advisory Council will conduct an inservice program on November 15, 1983, to increase the ability of advisors to work effectively with their advisee groups in the affective area.

The academic team members will share the activities which they have found to be effective with their advisee groups.

A committee formed by the Faculty Advisory Council will revise the T/A booklet to make it more relevant to the Webster T/A program as it has evolved since 1973 and more functional for each advisor's use. The first use of the revised T/A book will occur in the 1984-85 school year.

161

8. First-Year Implementation Activities and Monitoring Progress

The ideas gained from the inservice will be implemented on a trial basis during the remainder of the 1983-84 school year. Implementation will be monitored through the weekly minutes of each academic team and informal meetings and observations of advisors and advisees by the principal.

9. Evaluation

The program will be evaluated by members of the Faculty Advisory Committee through the use of the School Sentiment Index, advisor and advisee questionnaires, and observations by the principal.

10. Refinement

Evaluation of the program in general and of newly developed ideas will be done on an annual basis. A needs assessment will be conducted bi-annually to identify elements of the program that need to be improved.

11. Time Schedule

	Starting Date	Ending Date
Preplanning	September 1983	November 1983
Planning	October 1983	March 1984
Preparatory Activities	October 1983	March 1984
Baseline Year Evaluation	1982-1983	1982-1983
First-Year Implementation	1983-1984	1983-1984
Evaluation of First-Year Implementation	1983-1984	1983-1984
Refinement	1984-1985	Ongoing

12. Budget

1983-84 Consultants $250.00; T/A Manual writing $850.00.

Completed Project—
Increasing Teacher-Student Communication, 1984-85:
Franklin High School, Franklin, WI

(Enrollment 780 in grades 9-12.)

Persons Who Planned and Monitored the Project: Franklin High School Improvement Task Force--principal, vice principal, counselor, department coordinators, director of instruction, representative teachers, and special service personnel.

Goal: To help students with their educational, social, and personal problems and concerns.

Primary Implementation Activities: A "Let's Talk" program was started. In this program seven teachers are available for one period each day, a total of 35 hours per week, to talk with any student about anything the student wishes. Between 50 and 60 students per week talk with the teachers, about half of the total enrollment each semester.

Kinds of student concerns pertain to school rules and procedures, next semester's schedule of courses, participation in extracurricular activities and social events, academic problems, study skills, personal concerns, and peer relations. The teacher's primary task is to be available, to listen, to provide accurate information, and to help the student interpret situations objectively. Any serious problem beyond the skill or time schedule of the teacher is referred to a guidance counselor.

This program is an extension of the school's guidance program. The members of the task force regard it as highly successful and plan to continue it.

Chapter 10
Strengthening Home-School-Community Relations: Parents, Business, and Labor Participate

Rationale

Design Objectives

Preplanning Activities

Prototypic Plan

School-Community Activities, 1985-85:
John Audubon (Humanities/Fine Arts Middle School), Milwaukee, WI

Community Persons Coming To School, 1984-85:
Morse Middle School (Gifted and Talented Specialty Program),
Milwaukee, WI

Field Trips Into Community, 1984-85:
Eighth Street Middle School, Milwaukee, WI

Community Participation in Energy, Environment, and
Electronics Career Specialty Program, 1984-85:
James Madison High School, Milwaukee, WI

Community Participation
in Computer Career Specialty Program, 1975-85:
Washington High School, Milwaukee, WI

Rationale

Parents' attitudes toward school and education, their expectations about how much their child will profit from schooling, their supervision of the child's education-related activities, and the intellectual climate of the home are all related to how well the child achieves. The quality of the interactions between the parents and the school is another important consideration. Clearly, it is advantageous for the school to attempt to influence these factors in a positive way. An effective program of home-school relations accomplishes this.

Good home-school relations are especially important when any major educational improvement program is undertaken. The program is more successful when parents understand the program—its main features and how it is expected to better the education of their child.

One of the most reliable ways of influencing parents' attitudes favorably toward schooling is through their participation in individual conferences directed toward planning the child's educational program and discussing the child's progress and strengths. Another is through small-group meetings in which a teacher and parents discuss some facet of the educational program. A third is through parent membership on school committees. All of these are accomplished through an effective teacher-advisor program, a well-organized parent advisory committee, or both.

Effective schools establish good working relations, not only with the home but also between the school and the larger surrounding community. Individual teachers, counselors, and administrators bring community persons into the school and extend the school's educational activities into many community organizations and businesses.

Design Objectives

Comprehensive Objective

Effective communication and cooperative educational efforts between the school and the community are carried out as part of a program of home-school-community relations.

Illustrative Enabling Objectives

A comprehensive program of home-school-community relations:

Is formulated and monitored by a school committee composed of representative school staff, parents, and students.

Provides for frequent and effective communication between the school and community.

Encourages the school staff to become fully aware of the home and neighborhood conditions of their students.

Encourages parents and other community persons to participate in in-school educational activities and to provide suggestions to aid in decision making.

Involves parents in planning the educational program of their child and in monitoring the child's progress.

Involves parents in responding to school requests for their assistance in solving problems associated with their child's performances, such as learning problems, attendance, conduct, and the use of alcohol or other drugs.

Stimulates parents to encourage their child to attend school regularly, behave well, and try hard.

Provides for the child's progress to be reported to the parents regularly and meaningfully.

Preplanning Activities

The members of either the Educational Improvement Committee or a task force on home-school-community relations carry out the preplanning activities and develop the improvement plan. Other teachers, parents, students, and other persons are invited to participate in relevant aspects of the planning process. A district official serves as an ad hoc member of the task force or as a consultant to it. The preplanning activities take into account the district guidelines on home-school-community relations.

Members of either the Educational Improvement Committee or the task force carry out the following preplanning activities:

Study textbook Chapter 11, "Home-School-Community Relations."

Study other materials on "Career Education and Experiential Learning."

Assess the school's present situation, identify how improvements in the school's approach to home-school-community relations will contribute to improving the school's educative processes, outline possible means of implementing improvements in the home-school-community relations program, determine the kind of inservice education that will be needed, and estimate the costs of preparing for and implementing the proposed improvements.

Prototypic Plan

To enable the planning group to develop the improvement plan expeditiously, arrange the planning group's teaching schedules and provide substitute teachers as necessary so that the planning group can meet during regular school hours. As necessary, arrange for the planning group to meet outside school hours to gain information and to plan.

1. Area of Improvement

Increasing Parental Involvement and Support and Extending Educational Activities into the Community.

2. Need for Improvement

A needs assessment indicated that the parent advisory committee (PAC) is functioning quite effectively. However, only half of the parents are participating in activities that the PAC has recommended. Community persons are not participating as much as desired in educational activities in the school, and students are not participating in school-sponsored experiential learning activities in the community.

3. Percent of Students and Grades Involved

100% of the staff and students, and selected parents and other citizens.

4. Persons Who Will Plan, Coordinate, and Evaluate the Program

A task force on home-school-community relations.

5. Persons Who Will Implement the Program

All teachers, all counselors, all administrators.

6. Improvement Goals

General Goal--Parent-School Communication

Parent-school communication will become more positive as more parents participate in the activities for parents recommended by the PAC. (The PAC annually will develop a list of activities in which parents should participate. All parents will become aware of the year's activities designed for the particular parents by being sent a printed schedule early in the school year; their participation will be reinforced with a phone call from the PAC or the school early each semester.)

Performance Goals

90% or more of the parents will come to the school when requested and work constructively with the school on a problem that their child is experiencing and that the school cannot resolve without parental support.

75% or more of the parents who are not presently encouraging their child to attend school regularly, to behave well, and to try to learn will participate in a program designed to aid them in understanding the school's goals and requirements and the benefits of a good education for their child.

70% or more of the parents will attend group activities that are designated for them and will interact positively with the school staff.

90% or more of the parents will attend a teacher-student-parent conference each semester and will confer constructively with the teacher and their child.

90% of the parents will resolve questions or concerns they have by phone or in individual conferences.

General Goal--School-Community Relations

School-community relations will become more positive as more community persons come to the school as resource persons and as more students go into the community for programs of experiential learning.

Performance Goals

At least once per month a resource person or group will provide a program to each class that the class regards as worthwhile.

All students will participate in at least one experiential learning activity in the community at least once per semester and will regard the activity as worthwhile.

7. Preparatory Activities

Aid the school staff and PAC members in preparing to implement the in-school and out-of-school programs by leading the study of part or all of the correlated WRISE materials that the task force used earlier as a preplanning activity, arranging for the staff and representative parents to visit other schools and school districts that have exemplary practices, securing materials from schools and districts with effective programs, and arranging for other information-gaining activities.

Analyze last year's parent activities in terms of attaining desired goals. Modify, add, and drop activities based on the analysis. Prepare this year's schedule.

Identify the parents who last year did not attend scheduled events. Develop techniques for increasing their participation, starting with identifying schedule conflicts associated with parents' work or travel, single-parent conditions, and others. Adjust this year's time arrangements accordingly.

Analyze last year's involvement of community persons in in-school activities and of students' participation in volunteer, school-sponsored, experiential learning activities in the community. Modify or drop any that were not satisfactory. Identify opportunities for additional involvement of community persons in the school and of opportunities for students to participate in community programs. Develop this year's program in as nearly final form as possible.

8. First-Year Implementation Activities and Monitoring Progress

Implementation Activities

More Constructive Parent-School Communication

Activities involving parents are carried out as scheduled. Teachers, counselors, administrators, and PAC members use available means—telephone, mail, radio, TV—of informing and encouraging parents to attend their scheduled individual conferences and group meetings; absentee parents are followed up promptly. School staff

171

responsible for the activities ensure that parents who attend any activity are well received by the school and are encouraged to interact constructively with the staff and students.

More Positive School-Community Relations

Community persons participate in in-school activities as scheduled; students participate in community organizations and businesses as scheduled. The community persons, the students, and the responsible school staff carry out the activities in a mutually supportive manner.

Monitoring Progress

Once or more per semester, assess whether the scheduled parent participation and school-community programs are being attended as desired and whether the positive interactions are occurring as desired. Provide confirming information to persons for progress toward attaining the goals, and follow up with school persons, parents, students, and community persons who are not progressing as needed to attain the goals.

9. Evaluation in Terms of Goal Attainment and Effectiveness of Activities

The purpose of the evaluation activities that follow, and also of the preceding monitoring, is solely to improve home-school-community relations, not to arrive at judgments that influence teachers' or administrators' salaries or job security in any way. Accordingly, a task force member who is not responsible for evaluating teachers' performances coordinates the activities.

More Constructive Parent-School Communication

A record of the parents who participate in the scheduled activities and the frequency of their participation is kept. A questionnaire is administered to the parents and school staff to secure their perceptions of the worthwhileness and other aspects of the activities.

More Positive School-Community Relations

A record of the community persons who come into the school and of the students who participate in community activities is kept. A questionnaire is administered to the participating school persons, community persons, and students to get their perceptions of the worthwhileness and other aspects of the in-school and out-of-school activities.

10. Refinement and Renewal

A report is prepared summarizing the results of this improvement program. The report is prepared in such a manner that the results pertaining to any individual cannot be identified.

The cycle of goal setting, planning, implementation and evaluation will continue on an annual basis. Ineffective practices and activities will be discontinued while effective practices and activities will be maintained and strengthened. As the staff, parents, and community continue to engage in this cycle of activities and as more sophisticated staff development continues, the school will refine its capability for improving the education of its students and will experience renewal as a social organization.

11. Time Schedule

Chapter 1 has suggestions on developing a time schedule.

12. Budget

Chapter 1 has directions for budget planning.

School-Community Activities, 1985-85:
John Audubon (Humanities/Fine Arts Middle School), Milwaukee, WI

Community Representatives Coming To Audubon

Auditorium Programs and Related School Programs

    Friends Mime Theatre--fine arts/humanities
    Commander-in-Chief's Guard--humanities, history
    Robbie Clement--humanities, social studies, fine arts, music
    Hamilton High School--fine arts, music, band and orchestra
    Pulaski High School--fine arts, music, band and orchestra
    North Division High School--humanities/fine arts, black history, chorus, dance, and music
    Mr. James Cameron (author, historian)--humanities, history/literature
    Mr. Gerald Wallace (author, musician)--humanities/fine arts
    Reading Olympics--humanities, literature and "concern for the human condition"

Alverno College

December 1985

Planning session with deans and Audubon personnel for increased cooperative efforts between the two institutions

January 1985

Half-day joint faculty planning session for increased involvement of both faculties and facilities in the areas of critical thinking skills; dance, drama, music, and art; nursing; and community service, tutoring, and classroom aide

Second Semester

Ongoing contacts between both schools: nursing students working with exceptional education classes; college students tutoring Audubon students; planning for use of Alverno's stage and drama facilities for joint rehearsals and productions; and use of Alverno's conference facilities for Critical Thinking Inservice Workshops

Artist-in-Residence Programs

Muralist, stained glass artist, choreographer, and actors visiting and working in classes and both large- and small-group settings.

Other Resources

Project Business--community representatives from Wisconsin Bell Telephone, Delco Electronics, A/C Spark Plugs, etc. working with 8th grade classes discussing future careers and education requirements and explaining what the "world of work" is really like.

Parent Tutors

Parents tutor Audubon students in small groups or individual settings.

Project Upward Bound

Marquette University counselors visit Audubon students and counsel students for a program of pre-collegiate studies.

Guest Speakers

Mr. Gerald Saffold explains business opportunities to Audubon students.

John Gruhlke speaks in health classes regarding planned parenthood.

Norman Gill speaks on elections.

Barbara Bechtel shows slides on Russia.

Jim Cesar, Milwaukee Police Department, makes a presentation to the Drug Advisory Committee.

Lloyd Hudson, a reformed prisoner, speaks on social improvement of the humanities.

Annual Open House

Parents, relatives, and the community visit Audubon (1983 Open House was a Mardi Gras theme; 1984 was a Humanities Fair).

Annual Sports Night

Display of student athletic accomplishments and competition (student/faculty games and student all-star games, gymnastics demonstrations, aerobic dance demonstrations, pep band, etc.).

Annual Winter Concert and Annual Spring Concert

Parents, relatives, friends, and the community attend concerts of all levels of students' musical activity (band, orchestra, chorus, swing choir, dance groups, etc.).

Annual Awards Day

In honor of all levels of achievement within the Audubon student body (includes fine arts/musical productions).

Annual Completion Day Ceremonies

Parents, relatives, friends, and community honor our departing 8th grade students.

Annual Special Olympics Pep Rally

In honor of our competitors from exceptional education classes prior to their annual participation in the Special Olympics in Whitefish Bay.

Special 25th Anniversary Breakfast

Former faculty, students, and friends of Audubon commemorate the 25th anniversary of our opening.

Periodic Special Breakfasts

To recognize Honor Roll and other special achieving students.

Hosting the City-Wide Forensics Tournament

Over 500 participants in a secondary school city-wide tournament.

Audubon Going Into The Community

Fine Arts

Ensemble Noon Concerts presented in Alverno College cafeteria.
Band and orchestra trips to the Performing Arts Center's school concerts performed by the Milwaukee Symphony Orchestra
Annual Halloween Concerts--Audubon band and pompom squad perform in neighboring elementary schools.
"Nutcracker Ballet"--Audubon students go to the Milwaukee Ballet Company's annual production of "The Nutcracker."
Christmas Carol--8th grade classes go the Pabst Theatre for the Milwaukee Repertory's annual production during the Christmas season.
Milwaukee Ballet--7th grade students go the PAC for the performance of "Carmina Burana" and "Billy the Kid."
Audubon performing groups--band, orchestra, chorus, swing choir--visit neighboring elementary schools (Spanish class groups and aerobic dance groups also participated in these visits).
Chorus groups perform during the holiday season at the Grand Avenue, Southridge, and the main Milwaukee Post Offices.
Woodwind ensembles participate with the holiday groups.
Band and Orchestra participate in the Wisconsin State Music Association Contest.
Music students participate in the Milwaukee Jazz Experience at Alverno College.

Principal Avery Goodrich hosts parent-community meetings at the Vel Phillips Community Center.

Band and orchestra director Robert Davies and Learning Coordinator Patrick Doyle visit elementary schools throughout the city for evening PTA meetings, usually presenting an ensemble group (flute and harp) and then a slide show presentation of Audubon.

Guidance counselors Jerry Polacheck and Margaret McGinn visit elementary schools in the spring to counsel incoming students.

Audubon physical education teachers and exceptional education teachers annually coach, officiate, and actively participate in the spring Special Olympics held for exceptional education students. Audubon students each year also field a competitive team for these events.

Community Persons Coming To School, 1984-85: Morse Middle School (Gifted and Talented Specialty Program), Milwaukee, WI

Ministers of the Community--awareness activity.
WITI Weatherman--science project.
Firemen--lectures and slides, fire prevention (safety) week.
Minority Professionals--community awareness.
Aduna Si--presentation on African culture and dance.
Community Inner City Arts Group--presented play "The Bagman," educational drama.
Morse Parent and Community Organization--human relations activities, multicultural activities, Science Fair.
Senator Mordecai Lee--kickoff for student participation in project to restore the Statue of Liberty.
Hunger Project representatives--workshop for students on awareness of hunger throughout the world.
Rotary Club members, representatives of the Chamber of Commerce, Milwaukee School of Engineering--judges and coaches for Olympics of the Mind activities.
U.S. Navy representatives--career awareness.
Sheriff's Department representatives--career awareness.
Mrs. Marlene Cummings--black family life.
Ms. Sharon Durtka--information on China for 7th-grade unit studying China.
Hazel Weatherall (cosmetologist)--makeup demonstrations, home economics.
Benson Models--fashion, home economics.

Field Trips Into Community, 1984-85:
Eighth Street Middle School, Milwaukee, WI

Milwaukee Common Council--civic awareness.
Milwaukee Museum--research.
Central Library--research.
Milwaukee Safety Building--civic awareness.
Milwaukee Journal--career education.
Marquette University--community awareness.
Wisconsin Club--community relations.
War Memorial Center--community relations.
Grand Avenue Mall--community relations.
Jr. Academy of Medicine, UWM--career education.
Inroads--career education.
Upward Bound Program--career education.
Marquette University--career education.
Good Samaritan Hospital--peer counseling research.
Planned Parenthood--health education.
Wisconsin Electric Power Co.--science education.
NASA Space Exhibit--science education.
Oriental Theater--cultural awareness.
Ice Show--cultural awareness.
Tumble Brook Country Club--community awareness.
Shrine Circus--recreation.
Hamilton High School Planetarium--science education.
Museum of Science and Industry, Chicago--science education.
Kettle Moraine Nature Preserve--science education.
Pabst Theater--cultural awareness.
Centennial Hall--cultural awareness.
Riverside Theater--cultural awareness.
WMGF Radio Station--career education.
Mitchell Park Domes--career education.
Pathfinders--peer support counseling research.

Numerous field trips associated with extra-curricular clubs, teams, and groups.

Community Participation in Energy, Environment, and
Electronics Career Specialty Program, 1984-85:
James Madison High School, Milwaukee, WI

The Career Speciality Program (CSP) has an advisory committee. This Technical Advisory Committee is made up of individuals from companies that donate time, effort, and material toward the success of our program:

178

Mr. Taylor Benson, Marquette Electronics
Mrs. Rose Daitsman, UWM, College of Engineering
Mr. Dan Folkman, UW Extension
Dr. William Gentry, Johnson Controls, Inc.
Mr. William Heugel, Milwaukee Council of Engineering and Science
Mr. Tom Kavanaugh, Square "D" Company
Mr. George Kupfer, Milwaukee Health Department
Mr. Richard Meyer, Wisconsin Gas Company
Mr. Bruce Rubin, SE Wisconsin Regulatory Planning Committee
Mr. Al Stenstrup, Wisconsin Department of Natural Resources
Mr. Greg Vogt, Science, Economic, & Technology Center
Ms. Alice Wettstein, Wisconsin Electric Power
Mr. Bill Zabriskle, GE Medical Systems

This committee meets 3-4 times annually.

Our high school business partners are Johnson Controls, Inc., and GE Medical Systems. They have both provided many services to the school.

Printed brochures for Career Specialty Programs (CSP)--JCI and GE

Revised out slide-cassette series for the CSP program--JCI.

Provided a $50,000 grant to Milwaukee Public Schools of which a great part was spent at Madison for equipment for our electronics program.

Shadowing program--teachers were sent to JCI to see in person the job of a counterpart in industry.

Consultant and speaker service--experts from JCI visited Madison classes and shared their experience in our classrooms.

GE provided rulers for our recruitment campaign.

GE has provided a parttime secretary for the CSP during the busy recruiting and signup period.

JCI provided the staff at Madison a breakfast at the beginning of the school year.

JCI is providing incentives to students to be in school and on time.

JCI has provided summer jobs for the teachers over a six-week period.

JCI has provided an internship opportunity for a CSP student in their Quality Assurance Laboratory.

JCI has provided co-op opportunity for the business education students.

JCI is providing teachers 70% reimbursement for workshops taken successfully.

GE provided a workshop for a faculty group that is involved in supporting the students in the CSP.

GE provided a Youth Technology Award for students.

GE provided a plaque to the outstanding CSP student in electronics for the 9th and 10th grades.

GE and JCI have provided field trip opportunities for our students.

Numerous other businesses, in addition to our partners, contribute to our needs when they are asked.

Wisconsin Electric Power Company--booklets, films, field trips, speakers, financial support, etc.

Wisconsin Gas Company--booklets, field trips, speakers, films, etc.

Marquette Savings & Loan--field trip.

Industrial Towel and Uniform--field trip.

Central Methodist Church--field trip.

Plus others.

Community Participation
in Computer Career Specialty Program, 1975-85:
Washington High School, Milwaukee, WI

Twenty Milwaukee area businesses and educational leaders in the field of data processing developed the Computer Data Processing Career Specialty program at Washington High School in 1975 as one of the career options for students in the Milwaukee Public Schools.

Two major objectives of the specialty program are to provide students with an opportunity to explore computer related career opportunities and to provide beginning training experiences which are consistent with industry expectations for students where that career area is compatible.

The Board of Directors of the Milwaukee Public Schools instituted the specialty school program to give all students the opportunity to experience training in their chosen career area.

Business leaders participate on the Technical Advisory Committee of the Washington High School Computer Specialty program without students being aware of their involvement. This committee guides, directs, and helps mold the program into one that trains students for tomorrow's employment.

Introductory computer specialty students participate in a career workshop that includes representatives from the businesses throughout the Milwaukee area. The students interview data processing professionals to learn specific information about training, duties, responsibilities, fringe benefits, and work atmosphere of computer businesses in the areas of programming, operations, sales, technical support, engineering, and field service. This workshop generally provides students with an incentive to continue in their career explorations in data processing.

After the first year in the program, the students can be selected for different field experiences. Digital Equipment Corp. and Northwestern Mutual Life Insurance Co. provide field experience sessions for students to participate in data processing as it applies to their particular companies. The students visit the companies, learn about employment opportunities and requirements, tour the computer facilities, and participate in stimulating discussions with data processing professionals.

As students approach their senior year, they are given the opportunity to work in area businesses in the computer operations and computer programming departments. In 1984-85, 14 students were employed in Milwaukee at A.O. Smith, Northwestern Mutual Life, J.C. Penny, Wisconsin Bell, Master Lock, and Marine Bank. The business community has supported the specialty through these jobs since the program's inception. Some of the students who were employed as student interns during the seventies are supervisors of current student interns.

Most teachers involved with the specialty program are certified in mathematics/computer science or business/computer science. Since all of our teachers teach in two curricular areas, there are presently 15 staff members who provide a total of 38 daily classroom hours of computer related instruction. To date, eight of these teachers have been trained by private industry in the area of computer data processing. The training sessions for the teachers last from 11 to 18 weeks and provide the individuals with knowledge of today's technology. The Technical Advisory Committee, mentioned above, has been instrumental in obtaining placement for teachers in the training positions.

Chapter 11
Guiding Improvement Through Locally Conducted Research: Effective Schools Are Doing It

Rationale

Design Objectives

Improvement Research Method

Developing a Self-Improvement Capability Aided by Research, Burroughs Middle School, Milwaukee, WI

Developing a Self-Improvement Capability Aided by Research, Ashwaubenon High School, Green Bay, WI

Rationale

Progress comes through research. Through research we find solutions to current problems and also new means of advancing knowledge and practice. We improve the quality of education through research.

A school staff that carries out its own improvement research is telling parents and the public in general that, although we are doing many things well, we want to do better. We ourselves have good ideas regarding what might be better; we would like to try them out. We welcome expertise and cooperation from the district office and the university in conducting the research. But we want it to focus on our problems and interests, not on their questions or hypotheses.

Pause momentarily and recall the goal-based improvement strategy—assess current status, identify areas of improvement, set goals to be attained, plan to attain them, implement the planned activities, monitor progress, and evaluate the outcomes. This strategy is, in fact, a very powerful research method. Implementing it involves scientific inquiry, or research, of the highest significance for bettering the education of the particular children who attend a particular school—the children of your school.

This chapter gives information about improvement research, the goal-based improvement strategy. The dramatic gains made by Burroughs Middle School and Ashwaubenon High School in two years of implementing it are highlighted. Gains of these and eight other schools are given in a research monograph by H. J. Klausmeier, Developing and Institutionalizing a Self-Improvement Capability (see Appendix).

Design Objectives

Comprehensive Objective

Knowledge is extended regarding learning, instruction, school structures and processes, and other factors related to schooling through research conducted by school personnel and cooperating individuals and agencies.

185

<u>Illustrative Enabling Objectives</u>

The school staff:

Develops the capability for carrying out its own improvement research.

Participates with district personnel and other individuals and agencies in research specifically directed toward educational improvement in its school.

Participates with individuals and agencies in research directed toward extending knowledge concerning schooling.

Improvement Research Method

Improvement research was conducted cooperatively with schools and district offices in the late 1950s, and it has continued since. The method employed by the cooperating schools follows:

Assess your school's present status, its strengths and weaknesses, and briefly describe its educative processes. Retain the assessment information (test scores, teacher ratings, attendance, etc.) and the account of the educative processes before starting any new improvement project. These first data become the baseline year data against which to compare outcomes (and educative processes) each year thereafter. Thus, the data for each grade, for example, grade 7 or grade 10, of the baseline year are compared annually with the data of the same grade, grade 7 or grade 10, for each year thereafter. Changes in the data from year to year are related to the improvement activities that were implemented.

Based upon the interpretation of the data, identify areas for improvement and develop an improvement plan for each area, including measurable goals, activities for achieving the goals, and evaluation procedures for determining the extent to which each goal was attained and the effectiveness of the improvement activities.

Implement the activities and monitor progress toward achieving the goals.

Carry out procedures to determine the extent to which the goals were attained and to assess the effectiveness of the improvement activities.

As we saw in earlier chapters, the method is being employed successfully by many schools in attaining goals stated in terms of desired student outcomes, desired teacher outcomes, and improved administrative, advising, instructional, curriculum, and evaluation processes.

Developing a Self-Improvement Capability Aided by Research, Burroughs Middle School, Milwaukee, WI

(Enrollment 1,000 in grades 7 and 8 in 1983-84.)

Burroughs Middle School is one of 18 middle schools of the Milwaukee School District. The racial composition of the students in 1983-84 was 48% black and 52% white, including some Hispanic and native American.

Burroughs Middle School prepared its first school effectiveness plan for the 1982-83 school year and delivered it to the district office in May of 1982. The plan proposed improvements in (a) student achievement as measured by a norm-referenced test and a published criterion-referenced test, (b) implementation of the district curriculum guides, (c) school climate, and (d) home-school-community relations.

Achievement

Burroughs made dramatic gains in student achievement from the baseline year of 1981-82 to 1983-84:

MEDIAN PERCENTILE RANKS FOR GRADE 7 EDUCATIONAL
ACHIEVEMENT AND MENTAL ABILITY

	1981-82		1982-83		1983-84	
Subtest[1]	N	MDPR	N	MDPR	N	MDPR
Reading vocabulary	390	46.2	494	48.7	429	48.4
Reading comprehension	390	45.6	494	50.1	429	50.4
Mathematics concepts	389	58.3	489	64.3	421	64.1
Problem solving	389	57.8	488	58.2	417	58.2
Computation	390	65.1	489	65.5	419	65.9
Mathematics total	389	62.1	487	62.6	412	62.5

(continued)

	1981–82		1982–83		1983–84	
Subtest[1]	N	MDPR	N	MDPR	N	MDPR
Spelling	374	57.2	492	58.6	415	62.6
Capitalization	372	57.5		NA	414	62.9
Punctuation	372	56.9		NA	412	57.2
Language usage	372	51.6		NA	413	56.0
Language total	370	56.9		NA	411	61.5
Composite	350	55.6		NS		NS
Mental ability	342	52.8	443	54.5		NS

[1]Median achievement is based on May administration of Iowa Tests of Basic Skills, Form 7, Level 13, 1978. Boston: Houghton Mifflin. Mental ability is based on grade 5 administration of Otis-Lennon Mental Ability Test, Elementary Level 2, Form J, 1967. New York: Psychological Corporation.

NA: Test was not administered.

NS: Score was not provided.

We observe that the median percentile ranks were higher in 1983-84 than in 1981-82 in the 11 subtests of the Iowa Tests of Basic Skills that were administered both years. Six of the 11 percentile ranks were above the 60th percentile in 1983-84; four more were above the 50th percentile; and one, reading vocabulary, was at the 48th percentile rank. These percentile ranks, except reading, were above the median percentile rank in mental ability of the 1982-83 students when in grade 5. It should be recognized that the mental ability of the 1983-84 students was probably lower than that indicated for 1982-83. Only those students who were present on the day of testing in grade 5 and who continued in the school district from grade 5 into grade 7 are included in the group on whom the 1982-83 mental ability percentile rank is based.

The results based on the grade 7 standardized test may be examined in relation to the grade 8 minimum competency test results:

NUMBER AND PERCENTAGE OF STUDENTS MEETING MINIMUM COMPETENCY
REQUIREMENTS FOR GRADUATION FROM HIGH SCHOOL
IN APRIL OF GRADE 8[1]

	1981-82		1982-83		1983-84	
	Reading	Math	Reading	Math	Reading	Math
Percent meeting	56.1	40.0	76.1	48.1	77.7	50.5
N met	231	165	305	193	384	249
N didn't meet	181	247	96	208	110	244
Total	412	412	401	401	494	493

[1]Percentages meeting minimum competency are based on the students
who in April had taken the Basic Skills Assessment, Forms A, B,
and C, 1977. Reading, MA: Addison Wesley.

There was a large increase from 1981-82 to 1982-83 in the
percentage of students meeting the high school minimum competency
criterion in both reading and mathematics based on the Basic Skills
Assessment. The percentage increased from 1982-83 to 1983-84 but
not as much. However, if Burroughs continues the three-year trend,
the large majority of grade 8 students will meet the minimum
requirements in reading and the majority will meet the mathematics
minimum.

Indicators of School Climate

Information follows regarding indicators of school climate:

AVERAGE ATTENDANCE, SUSPENSIONS, AND FAILURES

	1981-82	1982-83	1983-84
% Student attendance	92	92	93
% Students suspended	21	22	21
% Failures	10	8	11

The average daily attendance increased from 92% to 93% from 1981-82 to 1983-84. This is excellent for a school in which the majority of the students are from minority groups. The percentage of students suspended remained constant; and the percentage receiving failing grades increased slightly. Hopefully, the percentage receiving failing grades will decrease sharply as achievement and attendance continue upward.

Other Indicators of Institutionalizing An Improvement Capability

The improvement committee of Burroughs Middle School responded to a questionnaire that included 34 items pertaining to the present design for developing and institutionalizing a self-improvement capability. The items were checked from 1 to 10 with 1 being the lowest possible rating and 10 the highest.

The committee completed the questionnaire in the spring of 1984 and responded for both 1981-82 and 1983-84. All of the items with a mean rating of 9.0 or higher for 1983-84 follow. The first number at the end of the item is the 1981-82 rating; the second is for 1983-84; and the third is the difference between the two years.

How many teachers of academic courses presented clearly stated instructional objectives to students? 8.50, 9.00, +0.50.

For how many students were the curriculum offerings and requirements appropriate (neither too demanding nor too flexible)? 8.87, 9.25, +0.38.

In how many academic courses were curriculum content, instruction, and assessment closely related? 9.11, 9.44, +0.33.

To what extent did the large majority of students receive instruction in each of their academic courses suited to their educational needs? 8.55, 9.00, +0.45.

On a typical day how many students were actively engaged in learning activities for nearly all of their class time? 9.11, 9.55, +0.44.

To what extent did the large majority of teachers and counselors aid students in assuming increasing responsibility for learning well, disciplined conduct, and governance of student activities? 9.22, 9.55, +0.33.

To what extent were school and/or district guidelines regarding student conduct made clear to students and implemented effectively by the school administration, teachers, and counselors? 9.00, 9.22, +0.22.

How often were students rewarded and recognized for exemplary performances such as high achievement, regular attendance, and trying hard? 9.00, 9.11, +0.11.

To what extent did the principal provide effective leadership by aiding the teachers in providing effective instruction, in securing good student conduct, in working effectively with parents, in gaining new knowledge and skills by participating in staff development activities, etc.? 8.66, 9.11, +0.45.

To what extent were you well satisfied with your job activities and interpersonal relations with other school staff, students, and parents? 9.66, 10.00, +0.34. (NOTE: Every respondent gave the highest possible rating.)

How many faculty members expected the students to achieve well? 8.75, 9.37, +0.62.

To what extent did the principal involve either a new or an existing group of teachers, counselors, and other persons in planning and coordinating the school's improvement program(s)? 8.55, 9.11, +0.56.

To what extent did the academic teachers use assessment information effectively to monitor student progress and to aid students achieve well in each course taught by the teacher? 8.33, 9.33, +1.00.

To what extent was assessment information of the current year used effectively in setting the school's improvement goals for the ensuing year and in preparing plans to attain the goals? 8.66, 9.33, +0.67.

To what extent did the principal arrange teachers' class schedules to enable groups of teachers and other staff with mutual improvement interests to have a common time during school hours for carrying out their preparation, planning, evaluation, and other activities? 8.00, 9.22, +1.22.

Based on all of the preceding information we see that Burroughs Middle School made remarkable progress from 1981-82 to 1983-84 in institutionalizing its self-improvement capability. Its organizational and support arrangements were already in place in 1981-82, and it made remarkable gains in student outcomes from 1981-82 to 1982-83. Continuing but smaller gains were made from 1982-83 to 1983-84 as student performances reached levels as high as could be reasonably expected, based on their entering achievement levels in grade 7.

Related to the organizational structures and support arrangements, Burroughs Middle School had a school coordinating council that functioned effectively during all three years. This council consisted of the principal, the learning coordinator, a counselor, and representative teachers. Nearly all of the academic teachers provided input to the council in the annual goal-setting/planning process that started in all schools of the Milwaukee School District in the second semester of 1981-82. During all three years, the academic teachers and the students were organized into instruction and advisory groups that included a team of academic teachers and about 120 students. The principal arranged these teachers' class schedules so that they, as well as the school coordinating council, had a common time each day during school hours for carrying out their preparation, planning, evaluation, and other activities. More than an equivalent of 20 half days were used each year for inservice/staff development activities, including part of the common planning period.

Burroughs Middle School implemented the goal setting-planning-implementation-monitoring-evaluation strategy very effectively the last two years. Having the students and academic teachers organized into instruction and advisory units enabled the teachers to implement the individual educational programming strategy informally but quite effectively, and to use assessment information regularly to monitor each student's progress and to encourage each student to achieve well, attend school regularly, and demonstrate disciplined conduct. It also permitted the teachers to implement the individual instructional programming strategy reasonably effectively with all students and exceptionally well with those scoring at or below the 39th percentile in reading or in mathematics on the grade 7 norm-referenced test.

Developing a Self-Improvement Capability Aided by Research, Ashwaubenon High School, Green Bay, WI

(Enrollment 1,093 in 1983-84 in grades 9-12.)

Ashwaubenon High School is the only high school in the suburban district. The racial composition of the students is primarily white and the socioeconomic level of the parents is average and above average.

Achievement

This high school started to develop an improvement capability in 1981-82 and formed its Educational Improvement Committee in 1982-83. The first comprehensive plans regarding achievement were developed in 1982-83 for the 1983-84 school year. The results from 1982-83 to 1983-84 are dramatic.

MEAN PERCENTILE RANKS FOR GRADE 10 STUDENT
ACHIEVEMENT AND MENTAL ABILITY

Subtest[1]	1981-82	1982-83	1983-84
Vocabulary	63	57	71
Comprehension	69	64	72
Reading Total	69	62	74
Mathematics concepts	68	65	77
Problem solving	76	71	81
Mathematics total	73	71	80
Language mechanics	70	50	74
Spelling	54	50	61
Language arts total	63	64	68
Reference materials	68	66	80
Survey of applied skills	74	68	76
Social studies	64	57	74
Science	71	62	79
Composite	68	64	75
Mental ability	69	64	74
Number of students	270	265	288

[1]Mean achievement is based on Science Research Associates Achievement Series, Level H for grades 9-12, 1978. Chicago: Science Research Associates. Mental ability is based on Educational Ability Series, Level H, 1978. Chicago: Science Research Associates. Tests were administered annually in January.

Mental ability and achievement in all except one area were lower in 1982-83 than in 1981-82; however, they were much higher in 1983-84 than in 1982-83. In 1983-84 the achievement battery and the mental ability test were administered in a more personalized manner, and the students were instructed in test-taking skills. A small part of the higher mean achievement may be attributed to these factors. However, the large part of the increase in achievement is attributed to the planned improvements that were made in the content of the various academic subjects and in the instructional methods and materials that were employed.

Indicators of School Climate

Ashwaubenon focused on improving attendance and decreasing discipline referrals starting in 1982-83, and it continued these efforts in 1983-84. The results follow:

AVERAGE ATTENDANCE AND NUMBER OF DISCIPLINE REFERRALS,
SUSPENSIONS, AND DROPOUTS

	1981-82	1982-83	1983-84
Average daily attendance	90%	94%	96%
Number of discipline referrals	3,000	2,118	2,150
Number of suspensions	260	152	135
Number of dropouts	25	25	18

Daily attendance increased from 90% in 1981-82 to 94% in 1982-83 and then to 96% in 1983-84, a truly remarkable gain. Despite this large increase in attendance, the number of discipline referrals, suspensions, and dropouts decreased markedly across the three years. These results are due to the planned improvements that were implemented in these areas. With respect to these results, the number of discipline referrals, suspensions, and dropouts might have been expected to increase rather than to decrease, inasmuch as the increased attendance was due in part to more regular attendance by misbehaving students and other students who were having difficulty in the academic subjects.

Other Indicators of Developing an Improvement Capability

Members of the improvement committee of Ashwaubenon High School responded to a questionnaire that included 34 items pertaining to the present design for improving schooling. The items were checked from 1 to 10 with 1 being the lowest possible rating and 10 the highest that could be assigned.

The committee completed the questionnaire in the spring of 1984 and responded for both 1981-82 and 1983-84. All the items with a mean rating of 7.75 or higher for 1983-84 follow. The first number at the end of the item is the 1981-82 rating, the second is for 1983-84, and the third is the difference between the two years.

To what extent did the large majority of students receive instruction in each of their academic courses suited to their educational needs? 7.62, 7.75, +0.13.

To what extent were the school environment safe and the classrooms free of discipline problems? 8.50, 8.87, +0.37.

To what extent did teacher education institutions offer credit courses and noncredit programs tailored specifically to meet the needs of the school staff for participating effectively in educational improvement activities? 7.75, 8.37, +0.62.

To what extent were you well satisfied with your job activities and interpersonal relations with other school staff, students, and parents? 7.87, 8.62, +0.75.

To what extent were school and/or district guidelines regarding student conduct made clear to students and implemented effectively by the school administration, teachers, and counselors? 7.00, 8.25, +1.25.

To what extent did the principal provide effective leadership by aiding the teachers in providing effective instruction, in securing good student conduct, in working effectively with parents, in gaining new knowledge and skills by participating in staff development activities, etc.? 7.12, 8.25, +1.13.

To what extent did the administrators and teachers share professional and personal interests and concerns and convey a spirit of enthusiasm and togetherness to the students and the community? 7.00, 8.37, +1.37.

To what extent did district officials verbally support the school's programs and activities to the school board, citizens, etc.; arrange for consultant and other personnel assistance; provide for essential inservice education; and ensure essential monetary support? 6.37, 7.75, +1.38.

To what extent did the academic teachers use assessment information effectively to monitor student progress and to aid students achieve well in each course taught by the teacher? 5.87, 7.75, +1.88.

To what extent was assessment information of the current year used effectively in setting the school's improvement goals for the ensuing year and in preparing plans to attain the goals? 5.37, 8.37, +3.00.

How often were students rewarded and recognized for exemplary performances such as high achievement, regular attendance, and trying hard? 3.62, 8.25, +4.63.

To what extent did the principal arrange teachers' class schedules to enable groups of teachers and other staff with mutual improvement interests to have a common time during school hours for carrying out their preparation, planning, evaluation, and other activities? 4.37, 9.12, +4.75.

The preceding results are self-explanatory. However, each item should be examined carefully and related to the goal-based improvement strategy, the educational and the instructional improvement strategies, and the support arrangements. The items with changes in ratings above 1.0 are especially interesting.

Ashwaubenon High School had developed a functioning self-improvement capability in 1983-84. It formed an educational improvement committee for the first time in 1982-83. An executive committee from this larger group was formed late in 1982-83. This executive committee planned, led, and coordinated the improvement activities in 1983-84, and it developed the 1984-85 plans. Most of the academic teachers provided input to the plan for both years. The faculty of Ashwaubenon High School continued to be organized in academic departments, and it did not have a teacher-advisor program. (Note in Chapter 9 that it started one in 1984-85.) Starting in 1982-83 and extending into 1983-84, teachers' class schedules were arranged very effectively so that those with mutual improvement interests had a common time during school hours for carrying out their preparation, planning, and other activities. The equivalent of 10 half days were used, including during the school day, for teachers to participate in inservice/staff development activities focused on attaining the school's improvement goals.

The goal setting-planning-implementation-monitoring-evaluation process was led and coordinated with moderately high effectiveness by the Executive Committee of the Educational Improvement Committee for the first time in 1983-84. The Committee used available assessment information effectively in setting the goals. Neither the individual instructional programming strategy nor the individual educational programming strategy were fully implemented in 1983-84. However, the counselors attempted to arrange appropriate educational programs for each student, and they used assessment information to monitor the progress of students who were experiencing difficulty.

The gains made by Ashwaubenon High School from 1982-83 to 1983-84 in all areas are as high as can be expected. However, it is possible that it will continue to make small gains in 1984-85 in all areas except attendance, which is about as high as possible.

Chapter 12
Implementing Improvement Processes
In Elementary Schools:
Successful Schooling Begins Here

Components of Effectively Functioning Elementary Schools

Improvement Plan—
Improvement of Mathematics Computation, 1984-85:
Parkview Elementary School, Cedarburg, WI

Improvement Plan—Improvement in Composition, 1983-84:
Thorson Elementary School, Cedarburg, WI

Improvement Plan—Staff Renewal, 1983-84:
Parkview Elementary School, Cedarburg, WI

Activities Planned To Increase School Effectiveness, 1984-85:
Auer Avenue Elementary School, Milwaukee, WI

Activities Planned To Increase School Effectiveness, 1984-85:
Richard Kluge Elementary School, Milwaukee, WI

Chapters 2-11 of this Guide are written for persons interested more in the improvement of secondary schooling than in elementary schooling. This chapter is for persons more interested in the improvement of elementary schooling. Chapter 1 is for both.

The first part of this chapter outlines the seven major components of an effectively functioning elementary school. All of these components must be considered in starting and institutionalizing a school's self-improvement capability. The next part of the chapter gives illustrative improvement plans—improving mathematics computation, improving written composition, and staff renewal. The last part of the chapter outlines activities planned by two schools to increase their effectiveness in several different areas of schooling.

Persons interested in elementary schooling should study Chapter 1 and then this chapter. Next, they should examine any of Chapters 2-11 to identify ideas that will help them with any area of improvement they may wish to undertake. It is important to recognize that much of the information in Chapters 2-11 regarding middle schooling is entirely relevant for elementary schooling. Also, the seven components of schooling and related concepts and practices given in this chapter are treated in detail in the earlier chapters having the same title as the components.

Chapter 1 is to be studied in detail because it presents an overview of a basic improvement strategy that is being implemented at all levels of schooling, a detailed description and an illustration of a 12-step planning process being used at all school levels, illustrative school district administrative structures and processes, district guidelines that are pertinent to all the schools of a district, and support for improvement at any school level. These critical processes, concepts, practices, and support arrangements are only mentioned in this chapter but are not discussed in any detail.

Just as it is well for those interested in improving elementary education to examine Chapters 2-11 for helpful ideas, so also is it instructive for those interested in secondary schooling to study this chapter. Continuity in curriculum and instruction and cooperation among the staff across school levels is a very important improvement consideration. Moreover, it is much easier for any school of a district to develop and institutionalize a self-improvement capability if all the schools of the district are stimulated and aided in doing so by the district office, supported by the school board.

Looking forward to the components of elementary schooling, recognize that the discussion focuses on improvement but that the improvement idea includes identifying and maintaining practices that are already effective.

Components of Effectively Functioning Elementary Schools

<u>Administrative Arrangements</u>

The elementary school principal, with input from the faculty, organizes the school's educational improvement committee (EIC). This committee is the key organizational structure for educational improvement. In some schools, it is an existing committee that adds educational improvement to its other activities, while in others it is a newly formed group. The committee is an integral part of the school's administrative organization.

Forming the EIC is the first step in starting the school's self-improvement capability. The committee is composed of the principal, representative teachers of each grade or team, and, in some schools, other staff. The committee represents all of the school staff that will be involved in implementing any improvement activity.

The EIC is responsible for leading and coordinating the school's improvement process as follows. The committee, with input from the entire staff and according to the district's philosophy and goals, takes responsibility for assessing its school's strengths and weaknesses, identifying areas of improvement, setting goals related to each area, and developing a plan to attain each goal. To insure successful implementation of the planned improvement activities, the committee monitors progress toward attaining each goal. Toward the end of the year the committee evaluates the extent to which each goal is attained.

This improvement process is explained fully in Chapter 1, and detailed attention is given to developing improvement plans. Illustrative plans are provided later in this chapter.

The principal, as leader of the EIC, insures that the following and other conditions are arranged to enable the school staff to plan, implement, and evaluate improvement projects successfully (more information regarding all administrative processes is given in Chapter 2):

Secures district office and community support of the school's improvement projects and creates a school environment favorable for school improvement.

Works out teaching schedules so that the EIC and other groups of teachers with mutual improvement interests can meet regularly during school hours to carry out their cooperative group planning, problem-solving, and other activities.

Provides the essential preparatory (inservice/staff development) activities that teachers need before implementing the planned improvement activities.

Provides the equipment, instructional materials, evaluation devices, and supplies that are essential for the successful implementation of the improvement projects.

Insures that classroom instruction is not interrupted by external events (announcements, unplanned visits, etc.).

Aids teachers in improving instruction, monitoring children's progress, and classroom management through regularly scheduled observations followed by individual conferences.

Provides recognition to teachers for effective teaching and classroom management.

Organizing Teachers and Children for Instruction and Advising

Excellent elementary schools pay attention to how students and teachers are organized for instruction and advising. The organizational format for instruction and advising sets a general expectation for role performance and for the informal interpersonal working relationships among the staff. It also affects children's interpersonal relationships and their opportunity for learning as well as the school's interactions with the children's parents.

In most elementary schools the teachers and children are organized into self-contained, age-graded classrooms. In other schools, they are organized into units of 3 to 5 teachers and 75 to 125 children. The teachers also serve as advisors to 15 to 25 children of the unit.

In the unit arrangement, the teachers work as a team to identify the content and materials of instruction and to determine the instructional and evaluation strategies each team member employs. They share information about their students and teach a class-size group individually or they share in teaching all the children of the entire unit.

In the unit organization, one teacher of each instructional team:

Chairs the meetings of the team.

Serves on the EIC and participates in the committee's planning and other activities.

Transmits information, decisions, and plans from the teaching staff to the EIC and from the EIC to the teaching staff.

Each team of teachers cooperatively:

Develops the procedures for planning, monitoring, and evaluating each child's instructional program.

Plans and evaluates the team's instructional strategies.

Related to the group's instructional functions, the teachers:

Outline the content to be taught.

Develop games, learning centers, work areas, and other aids to teaching and learning.

Plan the use of time, materials, and modes of instruction.

Participate in all aspects of the team's planning and evaluation activities.

Carry out their individual instructional activities in accordance with the team's plans.

Providing Effective Instruction and Personalizing Advising

Instructional programming for the individual student is a very powerful strategy for improving all aspects of instruction. Its focus is on the individual student rather than the classroom as a group. It is a three-phase strategy (see Chapter 4). First, the teacher plans an instructional program for each child during the first week of each semester and again later during the semester. The instructional plan indicates a list of the objectives in each curricular area that the child will try to attain, the type of activities and materials the child will use to attain the objectives, and the assessment tools and procedures that will be employed.

In the second phase, the teacher provides the learning activities that aid the child in attaining his or her objectives and regularly monitors the child's progress. As part of the monitoring process, the teacher confirms the child's correct performances, identifies specific difficulties the child is experiencing, and aids the child in overcoming the difficulties.

In the third phase of implementing the strategy, the teacher evaluates the appropriateness and value of the child's instructional program in each curricular area. The teacher uses this information in developing the child's next instructional plan. Based on the evaluation of all the children's programs, the teacher may formulate recommendations regarding changes in the curriculum, parent-teacher interactions, or any other aspects of schooling.

Individual instructional programming is not one-to-one instruction. Any child's program may include small-group and whole-class activities as well as some one-to-one. The strategy implies that there is no single method of teaching that is appropriate for all children and all teachers. However, there are some common features of effective instructional programming for individual children. These common features are relevant for teachers of self-contained classrooms as well as teachers in teams:

Instructional procedures and activities are carefully planned. Children are aided in getting ready for new learning activities.

What is to be learned and what is to be done (objectives and requirements) are understood by the child and instruction is focused on the objectives.

Unequal amounts of time are allocated to children of different entering achievement levels to attain the same objectives.

Different learning paths--instructional materials and activities--are provided to take into account each child's unique learning characteristics.

Different amounts of both teacher-directed and student-initiated individual, pair, small-group, and whole-class activity are provided to take into account each child's need for structure and preference for mode of instruction.

Printed materials, audiovisual materials, and direct experiencing are varied to take into account each child's preferred mode of learning--visual, auditory, or kinesthetic.

Each child's progress in learning is monitored carefully and children are aided in overcoming difficulties by reteaching and other techniques.

. . .

<u>Classroom management</u> procedures are carefully planned.

Teachers demonstrate their caring for the children and interact positively with them.

Rules regarding classroom conduct are understood by the child and are enforced fairly by the teachers and the principal.

Each child uses the entire class period in active learning.

Children are expected to learn well and achieve high in relation to their entering achievement levels in each curricular area.

Teachers publicly recognize children's high achievement, effort, regular attendance, punctuality, self-disciplined conduct, helpfulness to others, and other actions indicative of good citizenship.

Teachers demonstrate enthusiasm, fairness, and orderliness.

The principal and district officials provide teachers the conditions essential for effective teaching, support the teachers, and aid them in resolving problems of instruction and classroom management.

With respect to the advising process, whether in homeroom or a formal advisory group:

Each teacher serves as an advisor to a group of children.

Special education teachers, psychologists, and counselors work with children who have exceptional needs.

Each teacher meets with his or her advisees and their parents, as a group, to explain the advising process.

Each teacher conducts three or more individual conferences per semester with each child for the purpose of planning, monitoring, and evaluating the child's instructional program. Parents participate in two or more of these conferences per year.

Each teacher confers individually with his or her advisees regarding personal and social problems and provides small-group instruction regarding personal and social development.

Curriculum Improvement

Changing the content of the curriculum and increasing or decreasing the amount of time allocated for instruction in the various curricular areas are powerful means of influencing what children learn. Other means include changing textbooks and other instructional materials, instructional activities, and evaluation techniques.

The district office attempts to improve the curriculum of all the schools by developing curriculum guidelines. District curriculum guidelines are usually developed by committees consisting of representative teachers from each level of schooling and curriculum specialists from the central office. The district guidelines provide a structure that is intended to meet the common educational needs of all children, regardless of the particular school of the district a child attends. At the same time, however, the guidelines are adapted by each school and teacher to meet the unique educational needs of each child. A general strategy that local school staffs employ in improving their school's curriculum follows in abbreviated outline.

Each school bases its curriculum on the district's educational philosophy and the school's program goals. Course goals, course content, and materials and methods of instruction are in accord with the district philosophy and the program goals.

Each school focuses its curriculum on children's acquiring knowledge and understanding, learning skills or learning strategies, attitudes and values, and action patterns in the following programmatic areas:

Communication, including reading, writing, speaking, and listening.

Mathematics.

Science and technology, including computer technology.

Social studies.

The visual and performing arts.

Family and home membership.

Citizenship.

Related to the preceding areas, local school curriculum committees and individual teachers:

Identify or prepare content outlines.

Identify or formulate subject and unit objectives.

Identify or prepare instructional materials, including printed and audiovisual materials, that individual children use to attain their objectives.

Formulate instructional methods, including the use of time and materials, that enable individual children to attain their learning goals.

Ensure that assignments and lessons are neither too demanding nor too easy for any child.

Ensure that the content, the teacher's methods, and the teacher's assessment of achievement are closely related.

Establish procedures for reporting to the students and parents (and for ensuring a just and fair system of grading if letter grades are used).

Encouraging Children's Responsible Decision Making, Self-Discipline, and Citizenship

Parents and the public in general want elementary schools to encourage good citizenship. They want children to try to learn, behave well, respect authority, get along well with other children and with adults, and carry out other actions that are beneficial to themselves and to society. They want children with increasing age to make wise decisions and to become increasingly self-disciplined.

Wise decision making is learned (see Chapter 6). If students do not learn decision-making skills while in the elementary school, they will experience difficulties in the middle school. Similarly, if students are given no opportunity in the elementary school for exercising self-discipline and demonstrating other aspects of good citizenship, they will not meet these demands successfully upon entering middle school. Accordingly, elementary schools set and attain goals such as the following:

The children progressively assume more responsibility for learning well, self-disciplined conduct, regular attendance, and other aspects of good citizenship. In their classes and in meetings with their teachers they learn decision-making skills that help them to make educational decisions as individuals and concepts and skills that enable them to participate in shared decision making with other students, the school staff, and parents.

Each child exercises increasing initiative for making decisions and accepting the related consequences of the decisions.

The children as members of small groups take increasing initiative for making decisions and accepting the responsibility for the decisions regarding the governance of the class, attendance, conduct, and other aspects of good citizenship.

Responsible children serve as officers and participate as members of governing groups, such as the student council, and as members of school committees, such as school lunch or birthdays of national leaders.

In achieving the preceding goals, effective schools:

Foster a learning environment that encourages each teacher to try to meet the educational needs of each child and to take into account the child's learning characteristics, including entering achievement level in each basic skill area.

Recognize not only the highest achieving children but also those who consistently try hard and achieve well in relation to their entering achievement levels.

Recognize children publicly by displaying their pictures in the classroom and school corridors, posting their names and the nature of their recognition in the classroom and school corridor; having special field trips, luncheons, and other events for them; and writing letters to their parents.

Try to recognize every child for something at least once each semester.

Effective schools also develop written guidelines regarding discipline and attendance democratically, thus involving the administration, teachers, parents, and responsible older children. The guidelines are made clear to everyone--school staff, parents, and children--and are enforced consistently and fairly by everyone. The guidelines indicate what teachers do in implementing them and what district officials and the principal do to aid and support the teachers.

Discipline, Grooming, and Similar Items

Emphasize a child-centered, self-disciplined approach rather than a punitive, adult-controlling approach to conduct, grooming, and dress.

Recognize that each child's conduct, and misconduct, is a product of the child's attitudes and actions, the child's home/neighborhood conditions, and the school situation itself. Accordingly, make clear to children and parents what is expected and how the expectations are to be attained.

Carry out recognition activities pertaining to discipline such as the preceding ones for learning and achievement.

Work toward developing a positive self-concept in each child (see the activities of Auer Avenue Elementary School given later in this chapter) and constructive home-school inter-actions (to be described later in this chapter).

Attendance and Tardiness

Make clear to parents and their children that perfect atten-dance is expected, except for illness, and that the child is expected to arrive at school on time. If a child is tardy or misses school to share a business activity or a vacation with the parents, indicate the responsibility of the parents and the child for making up the work that is missed and the effects the absence will have on the child's grades and promotion.

Recognize good individual attendance with techniques similar to those given earlier.

Provide recognition to groups of children, such as those of a classroom or a grade.

Evaluating Student Learning
and Educational Programs

Principals currently collect considerable data as evidence of meeting state or federal standards. These data are usually com-piled only for complying with reporting regulations. A copy of the report is filed in the principal's office and the report is forgotten until the next year. However, in many schools, the staff uses the data to achieve higher student outcomes and to improve the school's educational processes.

A list of measurement devices widely used in elementary schools follows:

Teacher-constructed paper-and-pencil tests, performance tests, work samples, and observations. One or more of these devices is used in each grade from kindergarten on.

A standardized norm-referenced achievement test battery administered in at least two grades in either the fall or the spring.

Criterion-referenced tests, including minimum competency tests in various skill areas, administered in the fall and spring, starting in grade 2 or 3.

A mental ability test in grades 2 and 4 or 3 and 5.

Other measures of outcomes in the cognitive domain--creativity, writing skills, thinking skills, etc.--as frequently as desired by the school.

An inventory of learning styles.

Average daily attendance (annual).

Incidence of discipline referrals (annual).

Informal evaluation that is conducted without gathering and analyzing quantitative information is not to be overlooked. For example, the primary teachers getting together at the end of the first month of school to share their opinions regarding how well they are meeting the educational needs of the children can be more useful than studying test scores insofar as improving instruction is concerned. Similarly, the intermediate grade teacher may use part of the last week of the semester to secure each child's opinion regarding the worthwhileness and appropriateness of his or her mathematics or any other area of instruction, and the results of the evaluation are used in improving the educative processes of the school. Evaluation is interpreted to include pre-assessment, ongoing assessment, and post-assessment.

Schools use the preceding information in implementing each phase of the general improvement strategy that was explained in Chapter 1 and mentioned earlier in this chapter:

Assessing current status.

Identifying student outcomes that are satisfactory and that are to be maintained, and identifying other student outcomes that are to be improved.

Setting measurable improvement goals related to each area of improvement and developing a plan to attain the goals.

Implementing the planned activities and monitoring progress toward attaining the goals.

Determining the extent to which each goal was attained and the improvement activities were effective.

Evaluation information has many other uses including the following improvement related activities:

Assessing the extent to which individual children attain minimum competency objectives and other educational objectives.

Arranging an appropriate instructional program for each child.

Monitoring each child's progress in each curricular area to insure success and to avoid failure.

Evaluating the child's instructional program.

Making changes in the curriculum and other components of schooling.

Reporting to parents and to the school's educational community.

Effective Home-School-Community Relations

Excellent schools have established good working relations between the home and school as well as between the school and community. The teachers and principal have frequent contact with parents and other citizens. The school staff, parents, and other citizens work together in providing effective schooling for the children through a program of home-school-community relations.

A smooth functioning program of home-school-community relations:

Is planned, implemented, and monitored cooperatively by a school committee composed of representative school staff and parents and other citizens. A key element here is a parent-teacher organization. The organization includes the principal, a representative teacher and a parent from each grade or other unit of organization, and sometimes a school board member or other citizen.

Provides for frequent and effective communication between the school and community that enables parents and other citizens to understand the school's educational, including improvement, programs and enables teachers to understand the home and neighborhood conditions of the children they teach. Activities

214

designed to attain this goal include the P.T.O. distributing a school newsletter; conducting group events for parents and school staff for purposes such as overviewing an improvement project or recognizing children's accomplishments; carrying out a community fund-raising project; or surveying parents by questionnaire or telephone regarding some aspect of schooling.

Encourages parents and other community persons to participate in in-school educational activities. For example, parents participate in individual conferences with the teacher to plan the instructional program of their child and to monitor the child's progress. The parents respond to school requests for assistance in solving problems associated with their child's performances, such as learning problems, attendance, and conduct; and they encourage their child to attend school regularly, behave well, and try hard. Parents and other citizens come into the school for activities such as tutoring children; providing information to groups of children; and teaching children specific skills, such as playing a musical instrument. Other activities of this kind are indicated later in this chapter for Auer Avenue Elementary School, and middle school activities were given in Chapter 10.

Encourages teachers and children to participate in community activities. Field trips, visits to museums, and attending cultural events are common. Less common but equally important are school visitations to the homes of the children.

Provides for the child's progress to be reported to the parents regularly. Reporting progress fully and accurately is important for all children. However, it is critical for children in schools that have established a minimum level of competence in each basic skill area that each child must attain either to advance at the end of each grade or at the end of the last grade of elementary schooling. As indicated earlier, the individual conference is the only effective means for reporting this area of progress to parents. This is because the reporting must be detailed, indicating precisely where the child is in each skill area and what the teacher is doing to aid the child in meeting the minimum criteria. Homework and parent participation in aiding the child are clarified in these conferences. The school also reports to parents regarding the child's conduct, attendance, and emotional and social development. Similarly, the parents present information to the teachers. In this way, parents and teachers exchange information that aids them in educating the child at school and in the home.

Looking to the remainder of this chapter, we shall examine three improvement plan summaries and the planned school effectiveness activities of two schools.

Improvement Plan—
Improvement of Mathematics Computation, 1984-85:
Parkview Elementary School, Cedarburg, WI

1. Area of Improvement

   Improvement of Mathematics Computation.

2. Need for Improvement

   A needs assessment by the school staff indicated that some children were not achieving as high as desired in mathematics computation. A detailed analysis of the 1983-84 standardized test scores in mathematics computation showed that the achievement means of the grade 4 and grade 5 students were above expectancy, based on their mental ability scores. However, the upper quarters of each grade in mental ability were slightly below expectancy. Also, the achievement means of grades 2 and 3 were below expectancy, mainly because of their below-expectancy achievement in adding and subtracting whole numbers. Examination of the locally constructed criterion-referenced test confirmed these results.

3. Percent of Students and Grades Involved

   100% of students in grades K-5, except those classified as having exceptional education needs.

4. Persons Who Planned and Will Coordinate and Evaluate the Program

   Instructional Improvement Committee consisting of the principal, a teacher from each of three teams, K-1, 2-3, and 4-5, and two specialist teachers of reading and emotionally disturbed children.

5. Persons Who Will Implement the Program

   All K-5 teachers.

6. Improvement Goals

General Goal

   High student achievement in math computation will be maintained in the upper grades, and achievement in the primary grades will be raised.

Performance Goals

   The mean mathematics achievement computation score of each of the four quarters of each grade 1-5 in mental ability will be equal to or higher than their mean mental ability score.

The mean mathematics achievement computation score on the subtests dealing with <u>adding whole numbers</u> and <u>subtracting whole numbers</u> will be at or above the expected score, based on mental ability, in the primary grades (higher achievement on these subtests will also raise the total mathematics computation score).

7. Preparatory Activities

Meet within teams to discuss possible problem areas in the curriculum, use of materials, teaching techniques, learning activities, etc.

Hold cross-grade level meetings to discuss the preceding items.

Meet with teachers of other schools to discuss the preceding items and get suggestions on ways to solve some of the problems.

Summarize the ideas gained and determine which ones will be implemented by each team.

8. First-Year Implementation Activities and Monitoring Progress

Implementation Activities

Use the new techniques, ways of grouping, activities, and the materials as planned.

Increase the daily and weekly time spent on mathematics where appropriate.

Try to keep all the children on task during math instruction.

Continue to visit other schools to view their mathematics programs in action.

Monitoring Progress

Each teacher will regularly check the progress of his or her group and also of individual students.

Each team member will report progress and identify problems in regular meetings of the team.

The Improvement Committee will discuss progress and concerns at its regular meetings. The District Director of Instruction will attend some of these meetings and observe teachers' classes as time permits. The principal and Director of Instruction will provide assistance and consultation to the teams.

9. Evaluation

Each team will meet to assess the effectiveness of the new strategies.

The standardized and locally constructed mathematics tests will be administered to all children of grades 1-5 in the spring.

The Improvement Committee will examine the test data to determine the extent to which the goals were attained and to assess the effectiveness of the improvement activities.

10. Refinement

This project will be continued for several years, changing methods, materials, etc. as appropriate. The goal is to ensure that each child achieves as high as can reasonably be expected and that each teacher continues to refine his or her teaching competencies.

11. Time Schedule

1984-85 Preparatory Activities

    October. Teachers search for ideas and materials at the WEA Convention.

    October-November. Teachers meet in-house and at other schools to discuss instructional techniques, activities, materials, etc.

1984-85 Implementation and Monitoring

    October-May. Teachers try new techniques, materials, and activities.

    Teachers visit other schools and districts to observe other math programs in action.

    The District Director of Instruction observes Parkview math classes and as appropriate offers suggestions for improvement.

    January. The Improvement Committee meets to assess the program thus far and to offer input for the interim report to the District Improvement Committee.

The principal submits the required interim progress report to the District Committee.

January-March. Teachers continue to meet, to share information, discuss progress, concerns, etc.

April-May. Administer the standardized and locally constructed tests to all students in grades 1-5.

May-June. The Improvement Committee collects and makes a preliminary analysis of the current year's data.

June. The principal submits project report to the District Committee.

June-July. The Improvement Committee meets to make a final analysis of the 1984-85 data and to prepare the 1985-86 plan.

12. Budget

$350.00 - Extra pay to teacher committee members for time teachers spend during the summer of 1985 to compile and analyze evaluation data and to plan 1985-86 program.

$300.00 - Materials to aid math instruction in 1984-85.

$100.00 - Preliminary compilation of spring test data by clerical person.

Improvement Plan—Improvement in Composition, 1983-84: Thorson Elementary School, Cedarburg, WI

1. Area of Improvement

Improvement of Composition in grades 3, 4, and 5.

2. Need for Improvement

In a schoolwide needs assessment, the elementary teachers of grades 3-5 indicated that some children were not learning to write as well as desired. Standardized test results also showed some children achieving below expectancy.

3. Percent of Students and Grades Involved

100% of the children in grades 3, 4, and 5, excluding those classified as having exceptional education needs.

4. Persons Who Planned and Will Coordinate and Evaluate the Activities

The Committee on Individualized Instruction that includes the principal, the counselor, the reading specialist, and a teacher from each of three teams, K-1, 2-3, 4-5.

5. Persons Who Will Implement the Activities

All third-, fourth-, and fifth-grade teachers.

General Goal

Children of grades 3-5 will improve their writing skills.

Performance Goals

Children will increase the magnitude of vocabulary as indicated by the total number of running words used in a composition.

Children will increase the diversity of vocabulary as indicated by the number of different words used in the first 50 running words of a composition.

Children will improve the content quality of a composition as indicated by comparing the child's composition with other papers (holistic method).

Children will use a title for each composition and improve its appropriateness.

Children will write each paragraph in a composition as a group of sentences organized around a main idea.

Children will write a topic sentence as an expression of the main idea of every paragraph.

Children will improve in the accuracy of their spelling.

Children will use correct terminal punctuation in each sentence.

Children will capitalize the first letter of the first word in each sentence.

7. Preparatory Activities

Hold cross-grade level meetings to discuss the goals and to identify activities to attain the goals.

Visit other schools that are working on the improvement of writing skills.

Attend workshops and conferences related to improving composition.

Summarize the information from the various sources and identify what is relevant for this school.

8. First-Year Implementation Activities and Monitoring Progress

Implementation Activities

Teach the components of the K-5 language arts curriculum, **Written Expression**, giving special emphasis to the content indicated in the preceding performance goals.

Implement new teaching techniques identified through the preparatory activities.

Increase the amount of time given to the various aspects of written composition indicated in the objectives.

Attempt to keep all children on task during language arts instruction.

Return the compositions on the same day they are written if possible.

Point out errors the child has made and have the child correct the errors, giving assistance as necessary.

Continue to visit other schools to gain ideas.

Monitoring Progress

Each third-, fourth-, and fifth-grade teacher will regularly monitor the progress of the children.

Each teacher will report progress and problems regularly to the principal.

The teacher and principal will meet at least once per week to discuss progress and to plan.

The District Director of Instruction will observe classes and attend principal-teacher meetings.

The principal and District Director of Instruction will provide consultation and other forms of assistance.

9. Evaluation in Terms of Goal Attainment and Effectiveness

At least once per month, the teachers will meet with the principal and give their informal evaluation of the effectiveness of their instructional program.

All children will write a composition during the second week of October and another one during the second week of May. No assistance will be provided. Children will be allowed to use classroom dictionaries and no time limit will be imposed.

The compositions will be assessed by a panel of nonteachers (principal, Director of Instruction, District Reading Coordinator) using the Thorson School Composition Scale. The scale contains the scoring criteria, decision rules, and point values for each of the areas of composition included in this improvement plan.

The results of the panel's assessment will be discussed with the grade 3-5 teachers in a meeting before the close of the school year and the effectiveness of the various materials, exercises, instructional procedures, monitoring process, and principal and district office assistance will be estimated.

10. Refinement

This project will be continued into 1984-85 with modifications based on the evaluation. Further preparatory (inservice/staff development activities) will be provided as necessary.

11. Time Schedule

Preparatory Activities: August-September, 1983
Planning: September-October, 1983.
Implementation: October 1983-June 1984.
Evaluation: November 1983-June 1984.

Improvement Plan—Staff Renewal, 1983-84:
Parkview Elementary School, Cedarburg, WI

1. Area of Improvement

   Staff Renewal.

2. Need for Improvement

   Teachers informally indicated stress arising from the possible closing of one of the three elementary schools of the district and from other sources associated with this possibility. The stress appeared to be interfering with their enthusiasm for continuing to work more hours than required by the master contract.

3. Percent of Students and Grades Involved

   All of the teachers; no children.

4. Persons Who Planned and Will Coordinate and Evaluate the Program

   Committee of principal and six volunteer teachers.

5. Persons Who Will Implement the Program

   All teachers of grades K-5.

6. Improvement Goals

General Goal

   Promote staff renewal through more communication among teachers and individual and group means of reducing stress.

   Performance Goals

      Each teacher will gain a better understanding of the causes of stress and means of coping with it.

      Each teacher will indicate a reduction in stress from September to May.

7. Preparatory Activities

   Form a volunteer committee of the principal and six teachers to plan a program, attain the goals, monitor progress, and evaluate the results.

8. First-Year Implementation Activities and Monitoring Progress

Implementation Activities

Committee on stress summarizes results of inventory administered in the spring of 1983 and the fall of 1983, presents and discusses results in general terms at team meetings.

Hold rap sessions in Faculty Lounge to discuss school closing issues, facts, and perceptions.

Write to other schools for descriptions of their stress reduction and staff renewal programs.

Parkview teachers meet with teachers from the other two elementary schools to share ideas.

Collect articles from various sources for teachers to read and discuss.

Resource person addresses teacher stress in general in one session and specific issues identified through administration of an inventory in a later session.

Stress Committee summarizes means of stress reduction that may be relevant for individual teachers and groups of teachers of Parkview.

Teachers discuss the means in team meetings and rap sessions.

Teachers address sources of stress, such as use of coffee and cigarettes, family and teaching responsibilities and related conflicts, interpretation of events perceived as threatening, avoidance of some stressful situations, and sharing of stressful feelings and events with other teachers.

Teachers attend relaxation sessions conducted by another teacher.

Monitoring Progress

Stress Committee informally monitors progress through talking with one another and other teachers.

9. Evaluation in Terms of Goal Attainment and Effectiveness of Activities

Administer stress inventory in spring and compare results with fall administration.

224

Survey teachers to assess the degree of change they felt could be directly attributed to the improvement activities.

10. Refinement

Continuation of the program will depend upon staff response in May of 1984.

11. <u>Time Schedule</u>   <u>Starting Date</u>   <u>Ending Date</u>

Preparatory	September 1983	November 1983
First-Year Implementation	October 1983	May 1984
First-Year Evaluation	September 1983	May 1984
Refinement	Dependent on May results	

12. Budget

<u>1983-84</u>

$150.00 - Resource person
$100.00 - Materials

Activities Planned To Increase School Effectiveness, 1984-85: Auer Avenue Elementary School, Milwaukee, WI

All of the activities planned for 1984-85 related to curriculum and instruction in the basic skills, school climate, evaluation, and parent-community involvement follow.

<u>Reading</u>

The ultimate goal of the Auer Avenue reading program is to foster an appreciation for reading. The Auer Avenue reading program will facilitate the achievement of this goal by providing reading instruction and experience which assist pupils in developing their reading competencies through the assimilation of skills, concepts, and attitudes necessary for them to read effectively. The reading program will emphasize time-on-task activities that relate to increased achievement in all reading skill areas.

1. A comprehensive reading model will be provided for the staff.

2. A reading task force will be continued to review expectations in reading.

3. The staff will coordinate classroom/remedial reading services for Chapter 1.

225

4. Supplemental readers will be sent home for pupils to read to their parents.

5. A Hoffman Reader parental tutorial program will be established to supplement reading instruction for intervention pupils.

6. A systems 80 reinforcement center will be established in the IMC.

7. The staff will be actively involved in the assessment and monitoring process.

8. A Junior Great Books Program will be conducted for outstanding and interested readers.

9. Oral reading will be emphasized.

10. "Direct Instruction" and "Time-on-task" with related practice and application will be emphasized.

11. Reading skill instruction in other curricular areas will be emphasized.

12. Grade level expectations will be followed at each grade level.

Mathematics

The goal of the Auer Avenue mathematics program is to provide a balanced approach to developing proficiency in computation skills, math concepts, and problem-solving skills. Emphasis will be placed on math concepts and problem-solving skills. The Missouri Math Model, the Racine mini-math materials, and D. C. Heath materials will be used for instruction.

1. All pupils will master objectives for their grade placement as stated in the adopted Heath Math series.

2. The Missouri Math Program direct instruction will be followed.

3. A total content schedule will be developed.

4. Math Facts Cards will be sold in the office.

5. Monthly newsletter will highlight math activities.

6. Grouping of children based on ability, with the top group working above grade level when appropriate, and total content coverage by all grades.

7. Staff will set and review expectations in math.

8. Staff will coordinate classroom instruction with Chapter 1 math program.

9. Staff will be actively involved in the assessment and monitoring processes.

10. Reinforcement opportunities will be provided for the low math groups during special help periods.

11. Math facts will be emphasized.

12. Computer Assisted Instruction will be provided for eligible children in grades 4-6.

13. Homework will be assigned, collected, and corrected Monday through Thursday.

14. The administration will visit math classes.

15. Pre- and posttests accompanying the Heath program will be used to determine classroom progress.

16. Math facts will be reviewed daily and tested weekly.

17. Suggested home activities will be included in newsletter to parents.

18. Mini-math will be used to stress problem solving and review.

19. A primary and intermediate Math Olympics program will be held.

20. Grade level expectations will be followed by each grade level.

Language Arts

The ultimate goal of the Auer Avenue language program is to produce writing which is of appropriate quality for each student's grade level. Our program teaches children to write through active participation and stresses the process of writing. The Laboratory Approach to Composition Writing, the M.P.S. Grade Level Expectations, and the Macmillan textbook will be used for instructional purposes. Emphasis will be on the development of sentences, paragraphs, and composition in writing and of penmanship, listening, and speaking skills. Students will be expected to be good communicators by being able to listen, speak, and write effectively.

1. A local Language Arts Model will be used.

2. A highly structured, direct instruction model for teaching language arts will be used.

3. Forty-five minutes of direct instruction in language will be provided daily.

4. The Chapter 1 reading teacher will reinforce language skills in the Chapter 1 reading classroom.

5. Language classes will be visited regularly.

6. Grade level expectations will be followed at each grade level.

7. Selections of students' compositional and functional writing will be included in the parent newsletter and bi-monthly bulletin board.

8. Each child will get a chance to perform in a stage presentation.

9. Students will correct Daily Oral Language Activities daily.

10. Students will be tested each Friday on Daily Oral Language.

11. Awards will be given for outstanding compositions.

12. Three assessment meetings will be held. Students' language work will be examined by the Language Arts Specialist and principal. Specific findings will be made and discussed.

13. The staff will be continuously inserviced on the Laboratory Approach to Compositional Writing.

School Climate

Auer Avenue will develop a strong instructional program which will enable each child to be academically successful and therefore develop a positive self-concept. The interrelationships between staff and students will be stressed. Activities which will enhance a pupil's self-image will be developed and stressed throughout the school year. Self-reliance, self-discipline, self-control, and a willingness to excel will ensure our students' success in a wide range of life skills.

1. Attractive bulletin board displays of pupils' work will be instituted.

2. School spirit will be enhanced through the use of a school motto, goals, school colors, emblem, and tote bags.

3. Periodic assembly programs will be instituted with the students being the presentors and announcers.

4. The use of the magic words "Good Morning," "Good Afternoon," "Excuse Me," "Please," "Thank You," and "I'm Sorry" will be employed by all staff and students.

5. An honor roll and awards day will be held each semester.

6. A Student of the Week will be designated, 1st through 6th, including the Program for the Academically Talented and one L.D. classroom.

7. A Student of the Year will be designated, 1st through 6th, including the Program for the Academically Talented and one L.D. classroom.

8. A School Spelling Bee will be held in the second semester.

9. Students in all grades will own and use homework folders which should be taken home and returned to school daily.

10. A Career Month program will be conducted.

11. A Math Olympics event will be held.

Evaluation of Program Effectiveness

The staff at Auer Avenue School will continue to evaluate program effectiveness. We will continue to utilize a parent questionnaire and staff questionnaire to survey the perceived effectiveness of our program. Test taking materials will be used to improve students' test taking skills. The staff will also use standardized test data to evaluate program effectiveness.

1. Pupil progress in reading, math, and language will be monitored and assessed three times during the year.

2. A staff questionnaire regarding recommendations for improvement for the next school year will be issued at the end of the year.

3. Test scores will be shared with staff members and appropriate curriculum and instructional changes instituted to improve academic achievement.

4. A monthly report regarding children's reading levels will be perused by the principal.

5. An assessment of the implementation of the various policies in the Auer Avenue handbook will be carried out by the principal.

6. Task forces of teachers will be formed to review and improve various aspects of the Auer Avenue educational program.

7. Test taking materials will be utilized:

> Scoring High in grades 2 through 5.
> Mini Tests in grades 1 through 6.
> Indianapolis Test Readiness in grades 1 through 6.

Parent-Community Involvement for All School Components

Auer Avenue School will develop a broad-based structure of parent-community involvement in the school. Parents will provide assistance during the Book Fair, fund-raising events, P.T.O. meetings, a volunteer program, and tutorial assistance. Parents are always welcome at Auer Avenue School for classroom observation and parent/teacher conferences. Parents will also provide positive role models by participating in Career Month where parents and others come and share their careers with students.

1. A P.T.O. will be established.

2. A parent/student handbook will be provided.

3. A parent newsletter will be sent home monthly.

4. Parents will be inserviced as tutors for the Hoffman reading program.

5. A Book Fair will be held.

6. A Chapter 1 Parent Advisory Group will be formed and will meet regularly.

7. Parents will be invited for Awards Night each semester.

8. Test scores and testing procedures will be provided parents at appropriate times during the school year.

9. A parent questionnaire regarding recommendations for improvement for next school year will be issued at the end of the year.

10. A fund raiser for the P.T.O. will be held.

11. Parent volunteers will be inserviced to operate and staff the I.M.C.

12. Teaching teams will prepare periodic newsletters to parents regarding expectations, materials needs, and classroom rules.

Activities Planned To Increase School Effectiveness, 1984-85:
Richard Kluge Elementary School, Milwaukee, WI

Selected activities follow for this school.

Curriculum and Instruction

Provide a quality education for all students so that more pupils' level of achievement will be at or above appropriate grade levels, as identified by MPS, by increasing time-on-task in areas of reading, math, and language.

1. Strive to meet minimum grade level requirements in reading, math, and language:

   Review and discuss curriculum materials and grade level expectations at staff meetings and/or grade level meetings.

   Develop pacing schedules that will increase the amount of content covered and reflect high expectations for academic achievement.

   Plan for regular and more effective use of special help time.

   Include a writing activity as a part of each class's weekly language curriculum.

   Children above grade level may be used to tutor students below grade level.

2. Allow time in each grade's weekly program for social studies, science, health (including physical education), art, and music:

   Correlate or integrate subject areas to support each other.

   Incorporate special areas of emphasis (i.e., Black History, Law, etc.) into these existing subjects.

3. Schedule a specific amount of time (a minimum of 1/2 hour per group) for direct instruction per subject area in reading, math, and language arts.

4. Motivate children by relating lessons to real life situations (story problems in math).

5. Implement volunteer help to accommodate instructional needs in all content areas. (Recruit parents and students.)

6. Give homework which reviews and reinforces reading, language arts, and math instruction. Continue building-wide homework policy.

7. Provide individual pupil exchanges in reading and math, as needed.

8. Give students practice tests and instruction on test-taking mechanics in an attempt to improve standardized testing results.

9. Award certificate or other recognition to children for completion of reading books.

School Climate

Maintain a high level of achievement, attendance, and expectations for behavior.

1. Establish strong and consistent discipline rules uniformly enforced by all staff members:

   Administrator post and discuss rules in each room.

   Send copy of school rules to parents in September.

2. Emphasize use of positive reinforcement:

   Recognize academic and behavioral progress of all students (citizenship and scholarship awards).

   Continue school attendance award.

   Recognize good behavior (a duplicated form signed by administrator and passed out by teacher at least twice annually). Teacher judgment will be used as criteria.

3. Provide added activities to promote better school spirit:

Special Events Day	Dress-up Day
School Colors Day	Hat Day
Awards Day	Crazy Sock Day
Birthday Recognition	Rainbow Day
(card and candy)	Silent Reading Period

4. Encourage attendance and nontardiness by positive reinforcement as point systems, certificates, etc.

232

5. Instill a sense of responsibility in each child by encouraging purchase of needed materials.

6. Limit interruptions such as selective use of intercom at pre-determined times.

   Teacher announcements 8:00 - 8:15
                          2:00 - 2:15
   Student announcements 8:45 - 9:00
                          2:00 - 2:15

7. Establish a good attendance room award to be displayed outside the classroom.

8. Administration and staff will choose a monthly topic fostering attitudinal improvement.

   Implemented by classroom teacher and administrator.

   Teacher will lead discussion group in individual classrooms concerning this or other pertinent topics.

Instructional Leadership

Administrators should be directly involved with the instructional process, monitoring teacher performance and providing guidance and support to staff, and maintaining quality educational and improved behavioral standards.

1. Implement and monitor the Richard Kluge School Effectiveness Plan during the 1984-85 school year.

2. Continue monitoring teacher planning and strategies and pupil progress:

   Intervention conferences.

   Individual teacher/principal conferences concerning reading, math, and language progress.

   Classroom observations.

3. Increase involvement in educational process:

   Classroom visits for the purpose of building positive relationships between students and principal.

   Promote and enforce rigid adherence to school rules.

   Continue monthly newsletter.

Continue to acquaint new students and parents with the educational goals of Kluge School.

4. Support and cooperate with the Richard Kluge Science Center.

5. Review and update the Richard Kluge School Effectiveness Plan for the 1985-86 school year.

Appendix
Correlated Instructional Materials and Their Uses in Locally Conducted Inservice Programs

Secondary School Materials and Their Uses

Research monograph: H. J. Klausmeier, <u>Developing and Institutionaliz-</u>
<u>ing a Self-Improvement Capability: Structures and Strategies of</u>
<u>Secondary Schools.</u> Lanham, MD: University Press of America, in
press.

<u>Correlated Textbook Chapters, Guide Chapters, Filmstrips, and School</u>
<u>Experiences Audiocassettes: Wisconsin Program for the Renewal and</u>
<u>Improvement of Secondary Education</u>

The textbook, <u>The Renewal and Improvement of Secondary Education:</u>
<u>Concepts and Practices,</u> is available from University Press of America,
4720 Boston Way, Lanham, MD 20706. Phone (301) 459-3366. The manual,
ten filmstrips, and nine school experiences audiocassettes are available from CCL Document Service, Wisconsin Center for Education
Research, 1025 W. Johnson Street, Madison, WI 53706. Phone (608) 263-4214.

Guide Ch. 1: Implementing Basic Improvement Processes: Every School Can
Text Ch. 1: Introduction and Overview of an Improvement Design
Filmstrip: Introduction to the Wisconsin Program for the Renewal and
Improvement of Secondary Education

Guide Ch. 2: Administering School Improvement: Dynamic Leadership
Text Ch. 8: Administrative Arrangements and Processes
Text Ch. 12: Support Arrangements
Filmstrip: Administrative Arrangements for Shared Decision Making in
Secondary Schools
Audiocassette: Experiences of a Middle School and Two Senior High
Schools with Administrative Arrangements for Shared Decision Making

Guide Ch. 3: Arranging Total Educational Programs for Students: A
Helping Hand
Text Ch. 2: Educational Programming for the Individual Student
Filmstrip: Educational Programming for the Individual Student in
Secondary Schools: Part I
Audiocassette: Experiences of Two Middle Schools and Two Senior High
Schools with Educational Programming for the Individual Student:
Part I

Guide Ch. 4: Improving Instruction: Teacher Involvement Is the Key
Text Ch. 3: Instructional Programming for the Individual Student
Filmstrip: Educational Programming for the Individual Student in
Secondary Schools: Part II
Audiocassette: Experiences of Two Middle Schools and Two Senior High
Schools with Educational Programming for the Individual Student:
Part II

Guide Ch. 5: Updating the Curriculum: An Annual Priority
Text Ch. 4: Curricular Arrangements
Filmstrip: Curricular Patterns in Secondary Schools
Audiocassette: Experiences of a Middle School, a Junior High School,
     and Two Senior High Schools with Curricular Patterns
Text Ch. 5: Career Education and Experiential Learning
Filmstrip: Work and Other Career Education Activities in Secondary
     Schools
Audiocassette: Experiences of a Middle School, a Junior High School,
     and Two Senior High Schools with Work and Other Career Education
     Activities

Guide Ch. 6: Student Decision-Making Arrangements, Self-Discipline,
     and Citizenship: Democracy Includes Students, Too
Text Ch. 6: Student Decision-Making Arrangements
Filmstrip: Student Decision Making in Secondary Schools
Audiocassette: Experiences of a Middle School, a Junior-Senior High
     School, and Two Senior High Schools with Student Decision Making

Guide Ch. 7: Evaluation and Improvement Strategies: Using Information
     Constructively
Text Ch. 7: Evaluation and Improvement Strategies
Filmstrip: Evaluating Student Learning and Educational Programs in
     Secondary Schools
Audiocassette: Experiences of a Middle School and a Senior High
     School with Evaluating Student Learning and Educational Programs

Guide Ch. 8: Organizing Students and Teachers for Instruction: It's
     Time To Replace 19th Century Patterns
Text Ch. 9: Organization for Instruction and Advising
Filmstrip: Instruction and Advisory Arrangements in Secondary
     Schools
Audiocassette: Experiences of Two Middle Schools and Two Senior High
     Schools with Instruction and Advisory Arrangements

Guide Ch. 9: Personalizing Educational Advising: How To Combat the
     250:1 Ratio
Text Ch. 10: Teacher-Advisor Programs
Filmstrip: Teacher-Advisor Programs in Secondary Schools
Audiocassette: Experiences of a Middle School, a Junior High School,
     and Two Senior High Schools with Teacher-Advisor Programs

Guide Ch. 10: Strengthening Home-School-Community Relations: Parents,
     Business, and Labor Participate
Text Ch. 11: Home-School-Community Relations

Guide Ch. 11: Guiding Improvement Through Locally Conducted Research:
     Effective Schools Are Doing It
Text Ch. 13: Research-Based Educational Improvement

To be able to use the materials in inservice activities effectively, the staff development leader or leaders should be familiar with the design in its entirety and all the materials. They must (a) have a complete set of the materials and sufficient copies of each item to meet the inservice needs of the staff, (b) have essential projection equipment and facilities, and (c) have a plan for using the materials. Both the filmstrips and the audiocassettes should be previewed immediately before use by the leader (a DuKane projector can be used for both the filmstrips and the school experiences audiocassettes), and projection equipment should be tested to assure that it functioning properly and that the leader can operate it. Instructions regarding the projection of the filmstrip and the audiocassettes are provided in the printed guides that accompany these materials.

The materials may be used in several different ways in a school's internally conducted inservice program. The amount of material that is used and how it is used depend upon (a) the goals of the inservice program (b) the time arrangements that are worked out for conducting the inservice program and (c) the daily schedules of the staff. We now turn to these considerations.

Establishing Goals and Techniques of the Inservice Program

The inservice goals that follow are representative, not exhaustive.

Each staff member gains information about each WRISE improvement strategy and facilitative organizational structure and uses the information (a) to increase his or her knowledge of educational improvement, (b) to assess the school's current status and needs for improvement, and (c) to identify one or more areas for starting a schoolwide improvement program.

One technique for achieving this inservice goal is for an improvement committee member to lead either whole staff sessions or sessions for smaller groups of staff members. By this technique, the goal of the inservice program is clarified in the first session and the WRISE concepts and materials are introduced. The introductory filmstrip is shown. In the next sessions the leader typically introduces each component, introduces and shows the filmstrip, introduces and plays the pertinent segment of the audiocassette, presents key ideas from the text, and leads discussion. Interested staff members study the text between sessions, using the copies available in the IMC.

Another technique is for the inservice leader to organize the faculty into groups. The leader aids each group to become knowledgeable regarding one to three of the components. Each group then reports back to the entire faculty.

Each staff member gains information about WRISE components that can be implemented individually or by small groups without starting a schoolwide improvement program.

To attain this inservice goal, the task force presents an overview of WRISE to the entire faculty and then organizes teachers into groups according to their interest in areas such as adapting instruction more effectively to students' educational needs, improving evaluation, increasing student decision making and decreasing discipline problems, or establishing better home-school-community relations. After the groups are identified and time schedules are worked out, the techniques employed in attaining Goal 1 are followed.

Each staff member involved in an improvement effort that has already been identified by a task force with input from the staff gains complete information regarding the component or component areas to be improved.

This is a frequently occurring inservice goal and it is not as time consuming to attain as the others. To achieve this goal, task force members either use the introductory filmstrip to show the faculty how the area selected for improvement is related to the entire WRISE program or they move directly to the area(s) selected for improvement. Depending upon the size of the faculty, the proportion of the faculty involved, and the time available, the task force provides the inservice education to the entire group or to smaller groups in the same general manner as described earlier for Goals 1 and 2. The primary difference is that more use is made of the textbook since it contains helpful details that could not be included in the filmstrips or audiocassettes.

Each staff member new to the school gains an understanding of the WRISE strategies or organizational structures that the school is already implementing.

Many schools are already implementing one or more of the improvement strategies, such as teacher advising to promote the educational development of each student, or an organizational structure, such as systematic curriculum development. In achieving the goal, the improvement committee employs inservice techniques analogous to those employed in attaining Goal 3.

Time Arrangements for Inservice Activities

   Concentrated Workshops of 2-4 Days. In many school districts
workshops of two to four days can be conducted prior to the opening of
the school year, between the semesters, and after the students have
completed their last classes in May or June. Typically, the
participants are paid for part or all of these days.

   One-Day Sessions. Many school districts provide for one or more
teacher inservice days during each semester of the school year.
Typically, additional pay for the participants is not required.

   Part-Day Sessions. Some schools designate certain days as "Late
Arrival" and others as "Early Dismissal" for students.

   Teacher Preparation Period. Teachers are generally provided one
class period to prepare for their classes. Although this time cannot
be used for inservice activities, teachers can use it to prepare for
improvement activities related to their own classes.

   Other Non-Teaching Period(s). Teachers typically have a second
period each day during which they carry out various non-teaching
tasks. Some of this period may be allocated not only for inservice
but also for planning and for carrying out non-teaching improvement
activities such as advising students.

   Before/After Students Arrive and Leave. The school day generally
begins prior to the arrival of students and extends beyond the
dismissal time.

   Released Time. Through the approved use of substitute teachers,
aides, and student teachers and by teaming arrangements, individual
teachers are released from their teaching responsibilities, especially
for planning activities and curriculum development.

Daily Schedules

   The classes of teachers on task forces, improvement committees,
teaching teams, etc., are scheduled the semester before the group
meets weekly or more often. This is done to assure that the group has
a common meeting time. Often the teaching schedules are arranged to
free the first or last period of the day or the first or last period
before the lunch period thereby doubling the amount of time available
to the group. Careful scheduling also makes it possible for all the
members of most departments to have a common meeting time during
regular school hours.

District Use of the Materials in Inservice Education

Principals must feel comfortable about an improvement effort before starting it. District officials must judge the effort to be economical and effective before supporting it. One way to achieve these goals is for a district official and the principal of each secondary school to familiarize themselves with the program. This can be accomplished in a series of five or six half-day sessions.

To achieve the earlier goals, the inservice activities were led by a member of the school's improvement committee. The activities could be led by a district official or in cooperation with a district official. A desirable situation involves a cooperative effort by the local school and the district office. This kind of effort is enhanced when the district also has an improvement committee and has designated one person as the district's improvement coordinator.

Other Uses of the Materials

The materials may be used in other ways. For example, the district administrator shows the introductory filmstrip to the school board when securing board support for starting an improvement effort in one or more schools and for establishing an office of school improvement in the district office.

Parents and other citizens are shown relevant filmstrips to acquaint them with what the school is planning or is already implementing.

Student members of school councils and committees are shown relevant filmstrips, listen to audiocassettes, and engage in other information gathering activities.

Elementary School Materials and Their Uses

Materials

Klausmeier, H. J. 1985. Educational psychology (5th ed.). New York: Harper & Row.

Ch. 2: Aims and Objectives of Education
Ch. 3: Theories of Child and Adolescent Development
Ch. 4: Theories and Conditions of Learning
Ch. 5: Individual and Group Differences
Ch. 6: Instructional Theory, Technology, and Leadership
Ch. 7: Motivation
Ch. 8: Verbal Information
Ch. 9: Concepts and Principles

Ch. 10: Problem Solving and Creativity
Ch. 11: Motor and Vocal Skills
Ch. 12: Attitudes and Values
Ch. 13: Personality Integration and Classroom Discipline
Ch. 16: Evaluation of Student Learning and Educational Programs

Klausmeier, H. J., Rossmiller, R. A., and Saily, M. (Eds.). 1977. Individually guided elementary education: Concepts and practices. New York: Academic Press.

Ch. 1: Origin and Overview of IGE
Ch. 2: The Multiunit Organization
Ch. 3: Instructional Programming for the Individual Student
Ch. 4: Developing Mathematical Processes: The Elementary Mathematics Program for Individually Guided Education
Ch. 5: PRS: A Pre-reading Skills Program for Individually Guided Education
Ch. 6: The Wisconsin Design: A Reading Program for Individually Guided Education
Ch. 7: Measurement in Individually Guided Education
Ch. 8: Evaluation for Instructional Decision Making
Ch. 10: Home-School-Community Relations in IGE
Ch. 11: Facilitative Environments for IGE
Ch. 12: Continuing Research and Development

Lipham, J. M., Rankin, R. E., and Hoeh, J. A., Jr. 1985. The principalship: Concepts, competencies, and cases. New York: Longman.

Ch. 1: Determining the Goals of the School
Ch. 2: Organizing the School
Ch. 3: Providing Educational Leadership
Ch. 4: Improving Educational Decision Making
Ch. 7: Working Effectively with Staff
Ch. 10: Enhancing School-Community Relations

Using the Elementary Materials

The elementary materials are used in the same ways as the secondary. The important considerations are establishing the goals of the inservice program; having sufficient copies of the materials to attain the goals; providing capable leadership from the school, district office, or other source for each component of interest; and working out time arrangements so that the relevant local staff can participate at times when they are not already tired and worn out.

About the Author

Professor Herbert J. Klausmeier, University of Wisconsin, Madison, has taught at all school levels--elementary, middle, high school, and university. He is nationally and internationally recognized for his basic research on classroom learning, kindergarten through high school, and for his school improvement research. His improvement research first brought about Individually Guided Elementary Education, widely practiced throughout the United States and in Asian, European, and South American countries. His current efforts focus on aiding all schools, elementary and secondary, to develop a self-improvement capability. The enduring contribution of the self-improvement idea to the betterment of schooling is reflected in this book and in two other books, also distributed by University Press of America: Developing and Institutionalizing a Self-Improvement Capability, 1985; and The Renewal and Improvement of Secondary Education: Concepts and Practices, 1983.

Professor Klausmeier is unique among educational researchers in that he consistently validates his research findings and theories through cooperative research with the schools. The reader will find abundant evidence of the practical value of this approach in this Guide.

244